Educating America

101 Strategies for
Adult Assistants
in K-8 Classrooms

Educating America
101 Strategies for
Adult Assistants
in K-8 Classrooms

PADDY EGER

Tendril Press

Aurora, CO

Educating America:
101 Strategies for Adult Assistants in K-8 Classrooms

Published by Tendril Press™
www.TendrilPress.com
PO 441110
Aurora, CO 80044
303.696.9227
Educational & Corporate Quantity Discounts available

First Publishing: 2011
Printed in the USA

ISBN 978-09831587-5-2

Art Direction, Book Design and Cover Design © 2009. All Rights Reserved by
A. J. Images Inc. Business Design & Publishing Center
www.AJImagesinc.com — 303•696•9227
Info@AJImagesInc.com

To PCEP teachers, staff, students and parents:

a model of positive adult involvement

"Never doubt that a small group of thoughtful, committed people can change the world. Indeed, it's the only thing that ever has."

—Margaret Mead

Contents

Charts, Forms, and Tables

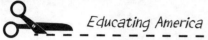

Preface

Everyday, volunteers make a difference in student lives. They assist teachers, work with small groups and individual students with two goals: to help students learn and to share their love of learning.

When our school began, we had two classrooms. Adult involvement was a cornerstone of our educational goals. Families joined because they wanted to be involved with their children rather than sending them to school. Each adult had strengths; all needed guidance from the classroom teachers.

Expecting the teachers to plan and deliver training for adults in addition to planning student lessons was overwhelming, but the teachers did both because both were important.

Year after year, the two classrooms expanded to include more and more classrooms and grade levels until we required our own building.

Classroom assistants continued to gain skills each year. Teacher responsibilities expanded. A decision was made to provide training for new and primary grade returning adults enmasse so everyone heard the same information. This book is a compilation of those training classes.

An interesting side benefit of the training affected classrooms beyond ours. Many adults enjoyed their in-class experience so much, they became district para educators. Others returned to college and became classroom teachers; some became administrators.

Educating America: 101 Strategies for Adult Assistants in K-8 Classrooms is a hands-on book designed for new and returning adults who work with students.

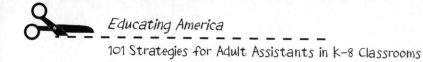

The chapters are arranged in sequential order, covering various stages from preparation to wrapping up work time. Charts, checklists and helpful ideas are provided in the book and through download from my website, *www.PaddyEger.com.*

Assisting in classrooms is a rewarding experience and a chance to affect student learning. Step forward. Be part of a growing movement of individuals investing in our country's education and our future.

Acknowledgements

Books require a village of professionals and friends to shepherd it through the planning, writing, editing and publishing process. Until I stepped into that arena, I had no idea how important so many people would be along the road to making this book a reality.

Special thanks and admiration go out to Linda Belz, my teaching/training partner and friend. We blended our skills and developed the training process that is the basis for this book.

Next, the PCEP teachers, staff and parents deserve thanks for helping us refine our ideas and making each suggestion user-friendly.

Fellow writers Ceil Higgins and Nancy Jo Jenkins along with my teaching and travel friend, Marilyn Melville-Irvine edited, asked questions and made suggestions. Each pushed me to clarify my ideas, inviting new people to step forward and volunteer to work with students.

When it came to publishing, Ceil Higgins provided a monumental nudge to get the book off my computer and into the hands of her friend Karin Hoffman, founder and creative director of Tendril Press. Then the work began in earnest.

Her team tolerated my endless questions and guided me from task to task until this book emerged.

Throughout the process, my family supported me, allowing me to forget to fix meals, answer the phone and be mentally-present for conversations.

To each and every one I give my heartfelt "thanks".

P. Eger

101 Strategies for Adult Assistants in K-8 Classrooms

Introduction

The focus of this book is adult teachers and the classroom assistants who support children day-to-day in our nation's schools. This includes supervisors, teaching interns, professional educators, para educators, parents and school volunteers who understand the "it takes a village" concept of teaching children. These people question the teacher who wants to be left alone to teach her students or the family that dumps off their children and says "Now educate them."

The intent of the book is to give all interested persons ideas to involve and train assistants for the mutual benefit of teachers, students and all adults. Throughout the book we will use the generic title 'adult assistants' to refer to all adults working in classrooms to support teachers.

The task begins with effective communication between teachers and adult assistants. Each must understand, trust and respect the other to work compatibly and effectively. Their combined efforts will improve classroom learning experiences.

Over the years, Paddy Eger's teaching colleagues, including myself and parents from her classrooms, have encouraged her to write a "how to" book on using assistants in the classroom. Paddy and I team taught for twelve years. I witnessed her daily success in integrating professional and volunteer assistants to enrich the education of students. She encouraged all to set high expectations and to assist students to achieve them. She developed small group lessons using the principles suggested in this book, and she modeled her expectations.

We would be less than honest if we led anyone to believe that implementing assistants into a classroom is "a bed of roses". It may look simple, but planning for and

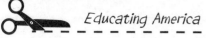

working with extra adults takes extreme amounts of off-the-clock time. Individual leadership skills, available times and interest in varied subject matter fluctuate from one person to the next. Some adults step in and feel comfortable while others express anxiety about working with students. If educators wish to avoid frustration from well-meaning adults, they need to provide basic training and share tools that will increase their assistants' successes.

In our own teaching, researching and volunteering experiences, we've felt our classroom was enhanced by our assistants, in this case parent helpers. Their presence in our classroom improved the quality of our teaching as we worked to improve the quality of each students' learning.

Over the years we read, heard and now believe that parent and adult involvement in schools enriches student learning and enhances student success.

Educators agree that home is the single most important factor in a child's education. Parents are children's first teachers. With that powerful information in mind, it makes sense for schools to encourage parents to play a strong role in the education of their children. Beyond insuring consistent school attendance, monitoring homework, reading with their children and attending parent meetings, parents who bring a love of learning to a classroom enrich the curriculum in ways a teacher alone cannot.

Our personal classroom program is part of a public school located north of Seattle, Washington. It is a parent cooperative that has over 85% parent/adult participation. This alternative school, a program of choice in the Edmonds School District, educates students from kindergarten to grade eight. While the school campus is located in a middle-class suburban neighborhood, families attend from the entire district with a base of

20,000 students, creating a diverse social, economic and cultural population. The bond that ties these families together is a strong commitment to active participation in educating their children.

In the Co-op or PCEP (Parent Cooperative Education Program), families must volunteer ninety hours of active support *per child* each year. Every family is aware of the commitment when they enroll; their assistance translates to ½ day a week for each child. These are dedicated people!

Classroom support from each family may involve the parents, grandparents, older siblings, family friends or extended family members. Most of their support is provided 'in class' with a few parents providing support from outside the classroom. Interestingly, every year, the Co-op has a waiting list of families.

During the 1995-1997 school years, I conducted research for a Master's of Education degree. My topic was "Best Practices and Parent Participation in the Classroom". The study did not reveal earth shattering information, but it did help the Co-op interpret information and experiences related to parent participation. From the information gathered and presented to the entire parent group, it became evident that a training program would benefit the school. That spring, parents voted to implement a required parent education program to begin the following fall.

Paddy and I designed the program during the summer. She became the presenter and received positive evaluations on the materials presented as well as on her mode of presentation. For several years each fall, she addressed new parents, prepared new information for returning parents and led discussions to share information at parent meetings. She also shared her ideas with other schools and non-profit organizations.

In my master's thesis research I was unable to locate any school with as highly involved parents as the PCEP. Many schools and classroom nationwide utilize or want to utilize more adult assistants in their schoolhouses. The success of our school depended on parents with no previous teaching experience. When we were able to give them strategies, their skills strengthened. Every teacher, student and assistant experienced positive changes.

Colleagues in other schools ask, "How can you stand all those parents around all day watching your every move? Doesn't it drive you crazy?" Our answer is simple: after working in an environment with trained assistants, we wonder how 'they' can survive without the extra support. But, until teachers understand the benefits to their students and are able to find the time to implement such a program, they won't understand what they are missing.

True, there is a certain amount of scrutiny by the adults, but mostly the assistants observe teachers to learn how they handle situations. By watching, the adults develop their skills. They lead small groups and work one on one with students more effectively.

Leading a small group of students may appear simple: arrive, work with the students and leave. This is far from the truth. Leading classroom groups is an enormous responsibility that takes preparation by both the teacher and the assistant. From the first day assistants enter the room, they begin an exciting and important task. Students look to them for guidance; they expect the adults to be organized and available when they need assistance. Students want to be productive and use their time wisely, and they give and wish to receive respect.

Whether assistants work with a pair of students or a group, several skills are needed to insure success. These include:

- Prepare to assist
- Set expectations
- Communicate effectively
- Expand questioning strategies
- Deal with misbehavior
- Develop thinking skills
- Monitor student progress
- Clarify details
- Wrap-up

The greatest obstacle in implementing a program where additional adults work in a classroom is *t-i-m-e*. Teachers are already overwhelmed by their commitment to their jobs. Adding another layer to training assistants, plan activities for them, and reorganize classroom schedules to accommodate those assistants is time consuming. The good thing about it is the *"give back"*; after assistants are added, they open-up more time for the teacher to work with individual students and develop enhancing activities.

Each school year, if teachers add one assistant each morning and another for the afternoon, within a few years the breadth of their curriculum will be amazing. Assistants provide the extra hands and help to gather materials, lead small groups, prepare enriching activities as well as manage day-to-day tasks. While this book does not promise a quick or easy fix, amazing things can happen when teachers and adult assistants commit their time to work together for the benefit of all students.

Linda Belz

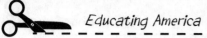

Prepare to Assist

Adult assistants perform an important role in the classrooms. They provide hands, help, and support for both teachers and students. It is a rewarding task if the assistant is prepared.

Part of that preparation includes attending a meeting/training session before you enter the classroom to understand the:

- Teacher's expectations
- Classroom organization
- Curriculum goals
- Discipline plan
- Suggestions for leading small groups

It is imperative to attend any and all training sessions provided by the school or teacher. Then, as other questions arise, write them down and schedule a meeting with the teacher outside student contact time. Do not expect to meet with the teacher unannounced asking for "just a minute" of time. Teachers' attention belongs to the students during school hours.

Focus on and understand the answers to these basic questions:

What is my activity and my responsibility to the students?
Who will assemble the materials I need?
Where will I meet with students?

7

What is my activity and my responsibility to the students?

Teachers vary in the way they plan classroom activities. Some explain assistant jobs ahead of time and may pre-plan the lessons for you. Others want helpers to be flexible and follow with the teacher's lead, then begin work with one student or supervise a random group. The teacher's work style dictates the approach.

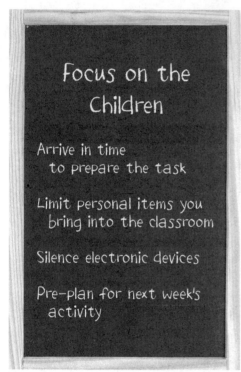

Most assistants appreciate specific tasks. They enjoy knowing the subject matter and may develop interest in adding extra background information or enrichment. Remember, whatever task you do, you are working to support the classroom, so be as flexible as possible.

Regardless of the teacher's preference, adult assistants need to enter the classroom focused on the children's needs. To that end:

- Arrive in time to prepare the task
- Limit personal items brought into the classroom
- Silence electronic devices
- Pre-plan for the following week's activity

It is best not to depend on the teacher to walk you through an activity. Allow yourself time to read the directions and gather needed supplies. Observe the current activities and the mood in the classroom. An assembly, a field trip, snow, rain, election of student council members or a class party may change the daily schedule. Change affects the environment and/or the time available for otherwise regularly scheduled classroom groups. Be prepared to amend the activity or use a "pocket activity" during your work time with the group.

Examples:

Today, all student groups are reduced from thirty minutes to fifteen:

1. In a writing group, share one part of each student's work such as opening paragraphs, favorite sentences or story settings. Discuss each student's strengths and then work on ideas for changes to enrich what each has written. This type of pocket activity supports the writing process.

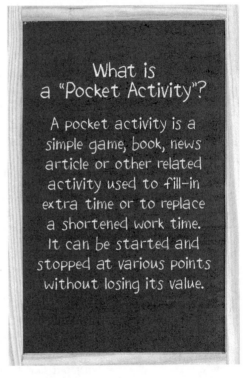

What is a "Pocket Activity"?

A pocket activity is a simple game, book, news article or other related activity used to fill-in extra time or to replace a shortened work time. It can be started and stopped at various points without losing its value.

2. The group task is to start a new story in the literature text and write questions for each other to answer. The story will take fifteen minutes to read, and ten minutes to discuss, plus it's Friday. Ask students to look back through previous stories to locate strong characters, favorite passages, best dialogue or some other reading-related observation. Discuss one or more of these with the group. Looking back and discussing features of previously read stories is a reading skill that incorporates compare and contrast.

3. Today is math quiz day. The quiz takes twenty-five minutes. Use your shortened work time to partner practice skills similar to those that appear on the quiz, or work to solve a math question from a supplemental math book. Practicing the math skills gives students a chance to check their understanding; working from a supplemental text will enhance the math group's thinking skills.

9

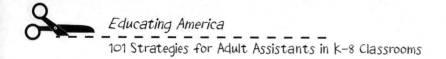
Limit personal items brought into the classroom.

The less brought into the room, the fewer distractions and the least number of possessions left behind. The short list of items commonly lounging unclaimed in classrooms includes car keys, coffee mugs, coats, electronic devices, umbrellas, checkbooks, knitting, novels, personal bills, plastic tubs with moldy food, jewelry, purses and warm-up clothes. By the end of some years the 'forgottens' could and often do fill a laundry basket.

If the teacher provides a safe place for your belongings, use it. If not, stash belongings in a bag or tote so your hands and the area around your work space remains clutter-free. Every stray item takes up valuable space, so plan ahead; leave personal belongings out of the room or stowed.

Silence electronic devices.

Come to school focused to assist students. It is best to leave electronic devices outside the classroom or on vibrate mode. Please, save all phone conversations until after your classroom commitment is over for the day or you are on break away from the classroom.

Pre-plan for the following week's activity.

The best time to prepare for next time is before leaving this week or, at the latest, a day before your next work period. Look over the next activity. Ask yourself: *What do I need to consider before I start the task? What could I bring to class to enhance student understanding of this next task?*

Example:

The primary activity you have just completed is looking for action words, verbs. Next week you are continuing with the same skill and are using a teacher-selected book of poetry which contains a high level of active verbs. You notice the verbs are words the children will enjoy acting out (jump, fly, scoot). Write down a dozen of the words to take home. Create an activity to "hook" the students into the task. Print each word on a 4x6 note card. Add a few non-action words like 'bus,' 'blue' or 'fun.'

Next week when you meet with the students, ask them to find action words in the poems. Next, show them the words you located. Ask the students to pantomime those words. When a non-action word like 'bus' occurs, students will realize they cannot act it out. All they can do is pretend to drive a bus so 'bus' is not an action word.

To extend the activity, have the students read other poems and watch for active verbs. Create more cards for the students to pantomime. This is a great 'break' activity for wiggly students learning to read!

For more information on enhancement see "hooks" in the Appendix and check out the author's 'blog' and 'discussion' on her website at www.PaddyEger.com.

Who will assemble the materials I need?

Decide what is needed to ensure an activity runs smoothly: pencils, paper, glue, specific books, art supplies, etc. Unless the teacher plans otherwise, collecting materials for student use is your responsibility. The longer you work with a small group, the sooner you'll anticipate their needs. Until then, consider the following details about support materials, copying materials and student supplies.

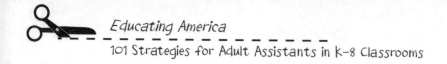

Support materials

Support materials can be as simple as a book about the topic or as elaborate as a museum-created educational box of artifacts. Your choice of enhancing materials must support the teacher's goals. All materials should be age-appropriate, user friendly and teacher approved. The goal is to spark student interest.

Select simple, touchable items. Allow ample time for passing and sharing the items; keep in mind that a specific task also needs to be completed.

Examples:

1. The group is learning to speak conversational French. (a) Bring Bingo Cards with colored squares for the students to cover when you say the color in French. (b) Play French folk music or (c) read a well-known short fairy tale (in French) sharing the illustrations as you read.

   Do not expect students to read words or listen to a long story when they are beginning to learn and speak conversational French. Sometimes a supporting activity may fill the entire group time. Check with the teacher before you plan something that extensive. Remember the materials are to support, not replace, the teacher-provided activity.

2. The local museum has boxes of cultural artifacts. Your group is studying people who live in cold climates. Bring in the box that shows models of Inuit homes, tools, photos from the 1930's and photos of current Inuit villages. Let the students handle the objects and photos. Discuss how Inuit lives have changed from the 1930's to today. Make a list of questions to research. After you put the artifacts away, read the social studies text about people who live in cold climates.

Copying materials

Know and follow the classroom and school policy for copying materials. In many buildings, teachers have numeric codes for their use of copy machines. If a teacher gives you the code, copy only the number of pages needed for your activity. Every extra copy made consumes reams of paper by years' end, many of which end up in the recycle bin. Never use school machines for private copies of recipes, cute cartoons or personal papers.

If the school uses a central printing site, allow a week for materials to be sent out, copied and returned. Be aware that most schools avoid copied work and focus on student-created pages and active discussions. Know the policies and ask for guidance with regard to copying materials.

If you copy materials, keep the originals in a folder and return them to the teacher for future use. Never give the original to a student who needs a new copy. Have another adult supervise your group if you must leave to make an additional copy. Better yet, teach the students to erase their mistakes and use their first copy.

Do not assume the teacher will prepare everything for you. Ask so you will know and can prepare ahead of time if necessary. If you are expected to create your own worksheets, check with the teacher periodically to be certain your ideas are on-target. Mark successful adaptations on your tasks with a sticky note attached to the original. Leave them for the teacher. Your changes may enhance future uses of the worksheet.

Student Supplies

Students may not arrive at your group with all the needed supplies unless the teacher has set that expectation. Pencils, paper, pens, scissors, tape, glue, crayons, paperclips, colored markers, rulers and sticky notes are often stored as shared supplies and are tucked away until needed.

For ease, organize supplies for your activity in an open tote. Place it on the floor next to your work space until directions are completed. Keeping key items such as pencils, scissors and papers off the table will reinforce student listening. Students won't be able to begin until the directions are completed since you have withheld the most important tools.

Expect students to handle and return supplies to you in an orderly manner. Give yourself at least five minutes for clean up before the end of your activity period. Then, use the last moments for a brief, "How did we do today?" evaluation.

Before you leave the classroom, return borrowed supplies to their storage area. Sharpen dull pencils, replenish paper and refill other items. If supplies are running low, leave a note for the teacher.

Where will I meet with students?

Nothing kills an activity faster than spending valuable time looking for a place to work. Consult the teacher prior to meeting your first group. Request a consistent meeting place if your group meets regularly. Teach the students to meet you there. This is easier than rushing around gathering them together week after week.

Establish an adequate workspace with seating for all, including yourself. The meeting place should be at least three feet from other groups. Expect the students and previous adults to leave the area clean and clear for your use. Personal materials should be stowed, not left hanging about haphazardly. The floor area should be clear of backpacks, jackets, book bags and other tripping objects.

Before students are instructed to move to groups, stand beside your work area so the students can see you. After a few times, they will remember where to assemble. If you need to adjust your location to provide space for a special activity such as a huge floor map, practicing a skit or working on a poster, the students will know to look for you, and will make the needed transition without your scurrying about rounding them up. This saves valuable group time.

Keep group voice levels appropriate so you do not interfere with other groups or activities. If the table location is crowded or you need to raise your voice above a quiet conversational level, relocate your group.

Teachers often display a chart to remind students of the appropriate voice level of 3-4 inches for their activity. If one is available, follow the guidelines. Keep a small one in your group folder. A sample chart can be found at the end of this chapter. A larger chart can be downloaded from the author's web site at www.PaddyEger.com.

Voice levels model respect for those in your group as well as other groups. It is vital to establish a quiet work ethic as most students are unable to concentrate when others are noisy.

Students who have trouble concentrating should be placed farthest from other groups as well as singers and chatty students in your group. Use "offices," three-sided cardboard dividers that stand up around an individual's work space, to create privacy and to block visual distractions. See directions on how to assemble "offices" at the end of this chapter, with a larger version and more ideas available at www.PaddyEger.com.

For some students, chattering or talking is part of the way they take in information. Accommodate their need to talk by asking them to read the directions aloud, give an example of what is to be done, talk with you privately, share an answer or tell the group how they discovered a new way to think about their task. During quiet work time, however, chattering students need to talk inside their heads or whisper if they need to vocalize words.

15

When you take time to plan before you meet with students, you ensure a better start to your activity. That means:

🍎 Understand the activity

🍎 Know your responsibilities

🍎 Assemble needed materials

🍎 Anticipate where you will meet students

These actions combine to establish your leadership and signal to the teacher and students that you are prepared.

Take Time to Plan

Understand the activity

Know your responsibilities

Assemble necessary materials

Anticipate where you will meet students

Voice Level Chart

- Level 0= silence
(testing, silent reading, working alone)

- Level 1= whisper
(speaking to one student)

- Level 2= quiet
(speaking to two people)

- Level 3= group
(voice only travels to members of the group)

- Level 4= class
(voice can be heard throughout the classroom)

- Level 5= recess
(active, outside voice)

Figure 1.1—Voice Level Chart

How to Build Student "Offices"

Some students benefit from having a private space to do their work. If space allows, build a few small portable "offices". Their use cuts down on student side conversations, copying others work and provides a specific, equitable space for each student.

1. Use 3 pieces of tag board, cardboard or sturdy paper.

2. Cut each piece 12 inches wide by at least 8 inches tall. (Any taller, and adult assistants can't peer in to check on progress.)

3. Join two shorter sides with tape, creating a strip with the 3 papers. The office is now 36" long and can be folded like an accordion paper for storage and opened to form a 3-sided (u-shaped) office during work time.

4. The back of each office abuts other offices or the work space of students sitting directly across the table. Therefore, students must keep their offices close to their own desk edge.

When offices are first introduced, everyone wants one. That will taper off over time. To accommodate everyone, point out that the space between 2 offices makes it's own office. The students offices abutting the offices on one side gain "office space" without putting up walls. It looks like:

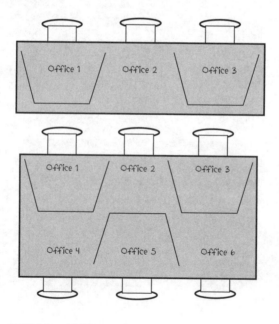

Figure 1.2—How to Build Student "Offices"

Set Expectations

To strengthen your leadership in a small group, understand your answers to the following questions:

What are my expectations?
How will students know to come quietly to my group?
Where will I sit for the best control of the group?
Where do I want the students to sit so they can focus?
Do some students need specific seating?

What are my expectations?

Your expectations must be in place before you meet students and must reflect those of the classroom and school; they exist to remind students how to act and contribute to a quiet work time with controlled transitions from group to group. Take your time and plan carefully. Most classrooms expect students will:

- Come quietly to the group
- Listen to directions
- Listen attentively to others
- Contribute ideas in an appropriate manner
- Work cooperatively

- Share materials and equipment
- Strive for quality work
- Work quietly and value others' work time
- Finish on time
- Help with clean-up
- Put away materials in an appropriate manner
- Wait to be dismissed
- Move quietly to the next activity

The first time you meet with a group, begin to explain your expectations. Do not read the list. Select four key expectations that will insure a measure of self-control and an equitable chance for all students to work and learn. These four are good for starters:

- Come quietly to the group
- Listen to directions
- Strive for quality work
- Move quietly to the next activity

Focus on the four you select. Explain why each is important and how the group will function when everyone meets those expectations.

Example:

"When you come quietly to our math group, we'll be able to start quickly. I'll give the directions, answer your questions and you will be able to start your tasks right away. If we work this way every week, at the end of our activity we will have time for math tricks from the book Mary brought."

Add more expectations each week. By the end of four or five sessions, it is likely all will be introduced, discussed and actively used. Be deliberate as you introduce them.

Example:

"In this group, we are working on individual math activities meaning you will work alone. I expect you to take out your own folder, read the directions and start your task. I'll be here to answer your questions. I expect each of you to work quietly, share the table space and the materials. After I check your answers, you may move on to the next activity."

After a school vacation or your absence for several sessions, reacquaint yourself with the students and review the expectations. These can be imbedded in your conversation with each group.

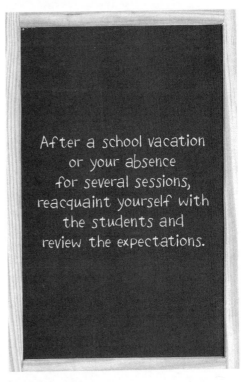

After a school vacation or your absence for several sessions, reacquaint yourself with the students and review the expectations.

Examples:

"Thank you for coming quietly to our math group today."

"Welcome back from the long weekend. Let's go over our expectations before we begin. I see you have all seated yourselves quietly, your eyes are on me and your hands are still. We have a great game today. After we discuss the rules, we'll play for the entire activity period."

Schools operate with a priority for learning grounded in respect and consideration for others. Adult assistants need to model this. Your comments and tone of voice demonstrate your regard for the students. If you are loud and silly, students may become loud or silly. Your goal is not to be their pal. Your job is to be friendly but firm and lead the group through each task. If you lose control to an unruly student, it may be difficult to regain a leadership role.

Classrooms with multiple assistants have variations in expectations. Students need to know your expectations; provide clues as you introduce activities and while they work.

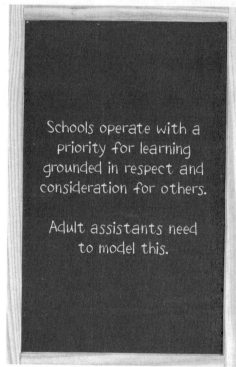

Schools operate with a priority for learning grounded in respect and consideration for others.

Adult assistants need to model this.

Example:

"In this group we will continue to work with maps and globes. Remember, we need to share materials and take turns looking for specific geographic landforms. Our voices must stay at a level 2 so only your partner hears you. When I place the globes on the table I want you to work quietly in pairs to locate a bay, a peninsula, and a gulf in North America."

A sample of small group expectations and student responsibilities appears at the end of this chapter and is downloadable from www. PaddyEger.com. If the list doesn't meet your needs, create your own; make certain to match both the classroom and school guidelines.

How will students know to come quietly to my group?

If the expectation for students is to arrive quietly to your group is not in place, it won't happen. You must let them know what is acceptable by modeling or reminding them how to approach your group from a previous activity.

Example:

"When you come to this group, I expect you to look first. Be certain the previous group has been excused. I will invite you to sit down after I have everything ready. Next, quietly pull out your chair, sit down and wait for my directions.

"I expect that you will not touch anything on the table until we have discussed our activity for today."

If students come to the group clowning around or getting noisy, redirect their attention. Include your expectations as you get started.

Examples:

"I like the way Mary arrived quietly to our group today."

"I noticed that you all stopped and waited until I was ready for you."

"We can do a better job of moving quietly. Please stand and let's pretend you are arriving. Show me 2 things: first, how quietly you can sit down; second, show me how I will know you are ready to listen."

When students are ready, reinforce how well they met your expectations. Restate what they have done well in a simple statement of praise.

Example:

"Good job. You remembered how to come quietly to our group. Let's get started on today's tasks."

Student behavior adjusts as you restate your expectations. Hands get quiet, voices turn off and students look around to see if others are doing what you have requested. Don't discount the power of praise.

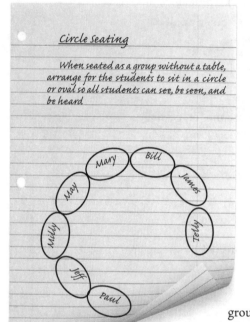

Circle Seating

When seated as a group without a table, arrange for the students to sit in a circle or oval so all students can see, be seen, and be heard

Where will I sit for the best control of the group?

The end of a rectangular table is *not* the best place to sit. It is too removed from the students at the other end of the table. Sit in the middle seat along one side of the table where you can see all students, reach out to touch each student's work, as well as become part of the group. Sitting on one side allows you to speak in a softer voice and creates a more intimate group. Best of all, you can keep an eye on student progress (especially if you can read upside down!).

If you use a round table, seat the students to focus them away from nearby groups, leaving you facing neighboring tables. Round tables present a problem; you are farther from all students and must use a stronger voice. To help with control, you may need to stand when you give directions. Be careful to avoid talking to the backs of students. Later, during the activity time, walk around the group and monitor individual progress.

When seated as a group without a table, arrange for the students to sit in a circle or oval so all students can see, be seen, and be heard. Keep the group seated as close together as possible so voice levels remain as low as possible. During work time, walk behind the students and look over their shoulders to check their progress.

To keep track of student names in each group, make a chart showing the order in which they are seated. Use the chart to record which students have been called on. Jot down concerns about student successes, frustrations, behavior and possible questions that come to mind. Turn in the chart to the teacher before leaving school.

Read the markings and comments on the simulation to the right for ideas on how you might keep track of information in a concise manner.

The "–" means students were off-task, "+" means students contributed well. The "?" indicates you are not sure if the student understands the concepts. Information in parentheses reflects your impression of the student's contribution to the group.

If the group exceeds eight students, you may need to work in a different way to keep voice levels lower. Assign the students to work in pairs with the person seated next to them. Give each pair a pertinent question or problem. They can share their thoughts and work together to find the best solution.

After an appropriate amount of time, have each pair share their combined results with the group. Lead a discussion including each pairs' findings.

Markings and Comments
Mary - - ? (slow to process this concept)
Bill - + + (detailed answers)
May + + - (bossy today)
Milly ?? (left for speech class)
Jeff + + (understands lesson today)
Tom - (too much to read)
Telly - - ? (distracted)
James + + + (interrupts others)
Paul + ?? (left early for speech)

Example:

Today your group of nine is reading a social studies text about early explorers. Give each pair a section of the text to read, discuss together and report back to the group.

"Team One, read the section about the countries that sent out explorers from 1500 to 1600. List the countries, their rulers and the explorers they sent out. Select the three most important facts about why they sent out explorers.

"Team Two, chart the various explorers mentioned in Section Three. Show the countries they left from, when they left, where they explored and when they returned.

"Team Three, use the laminated map and chart out the common routes the explorers used. Vary the colors and write a key to help us identify their routes.

"Team Four, you will have three people. Read Section Five. List the various products and treasures the explorers brought back to their home country. Decide how you think each "find" affected future explorations. Report the success of their explorations."

With large groups, you can also divide up the tasks to prepare for experiments and other multi-part activities. The students will be actively involved and, with them taking on the varied tasks, you act as a coordinator.

Example:

"Today we will work in pairs to get organized for our experiment using the various types of rocks in the science kit. Listen for your tasks. Pair One, list the five steps we need to complete the experiment on the white board. Pair Two, make a list of materials we will need. Pair Three, choose the three most important questions we need to answer today. Pair Four, today you will wait quietly then assemble the materials Pair Two lists for you. Pair Five you will oversee group clean-up."

Take a few minutes to organize a larger group; it saves time and keeps students engaged, creating a better chance of completing the task. Remember, the students need to do the task and clean up. You are their guide.

Where do I want the students to sit so they can focus?

Consider the location of distractions such as the TV, computers, windows, active groups, doors, sinks and supply areas. Most adult assistants can face distractions and remain focused; many students find such distractions difficult to handle.

Position the group for their best listening and learning. Move students to face away from a TV program or computer; seat them so the glare from windows is at their backs. Block other distractions with a large paper, screen, or poster.

Talk with the teacher if space or distraction problems interfere with your task. The best solution would be to move the group to another location with fewer distractions. Remember, your goal is to complete your activity in an appropriate and timely manner.

Take a few minutes to organize a larger group; it saves time and keeps students engaged, creating a better chance of completing the task.

Do some students need specific seating?

Students with visual, hearing, movement or behavior issues may need adaptation for activities. If so, assign seats for all students in the group to keep from singling out a few. Review the new seating and make adjustments as needed. Some groups need to be shifted if students become 'too comfortable' with their seat mates and begin to lose focus.

Students have varying ways of taking in information. Try to accommodate their needs. Maybe Mary needs to see the book up close or James needs more space because he moves around as he

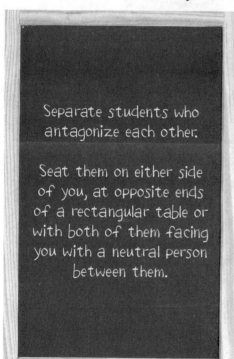

Separate students who antagonize each other.

Seat them on either side of you, at opposite ends of a rectangular table or with both of them facing you with a neutral person between them.

works. Talk with the group about how all people have different needs. Students will accommodate their peers needs as long as their personal needs are not being ignored.

Separate students who antagonize each other. Seat them on either side of you, at opposite ends of a rectangular table or with both of them facing you with a neutral person between them. If they sit facing you, it will be easier to keep track of their movements and interactions. Avoid seating them directly across from each other at a narrow table; they may continue disruptive behavior under the table with their feet.

Expect all students to follow the guidelines unless told otherwise by the teacher. Know how you will handle aggressive situations before you start a group. Using praise for their positive qualities goes a long way to earn their respect and cooperation. Later, if you need to remind them about their behavior, they will be more receptive because they have received your positive feedback.

If a student has behavioral needs or if you have serious difficulties with a particular student, it is best to discuss modifications with the teacher prior to changing expectations for that student. If a student continues to act out or is unable to complete a task, consult the teacher for additional modifications. She has responsibility for behavioral decisions in accordance with school and district policies.

Remember, seeking help is not a sign of weakness. Discussing a behavior problem or a situation with the teacher demonstrates your awareness and concern. Unchecked situations, glossing over small group expectations, or not following through on expectations may create problems that affect the group's ability to complete a task. It is easier to set firm expectations early on than to try to go back and set firm expectations later in the year.

When students have special needs, all related information is confidential and should never be discussed with anyone but the teacher. Parents, students, other teachers, your neighbors and your cat don't need to know about a student's problems. Respect confidentiality.

If you lay out a plan that explains your goals for student responsibility, you will maintain more control of the group. When students have a clear understanding of your expectations, they are more likely to comply. Use the school's plan. If one doesn't exist, share the sample plan at the end of this chapter or download it from www.PaddyEger.com

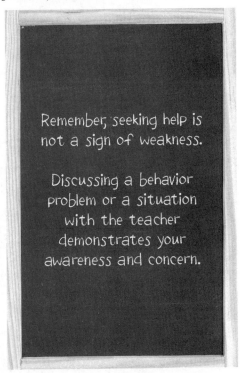

Remember, seeking help is not a sign of weakness.

Discussing a behavior problem or a situation with the teacher demonstrates your awareness and concern.

Expectations for Students

- Come quietly to the group.
- Listen to directions.
- Listen attentively to others.
- Contribute ideas appropriately.
- Work cooperatively.
- Share materials and equipment.
- Strive for quality work.
- Work quietly and value others' work time.
- Finish on time.
- Help with clean-up.
- Put away materials appropriately.
- Wait to be dismissed.
- Move quietly to the next activity.

Figure 2.1—Expectations for Students

Student Responsibilities
in Small Groups

Arriving

1. Join the group quietly.
2. Wait to be invited to sit.
3. Sit down quietly.
4. Give the adult leader your attention.
5. Engage your brain.
6. Listen to group discussions.
7. Participate in discussions.
8. Ask questions to clarify tasks.

LEAVING

1. Listen to the adult.
2. Stop working when asked.
3. Turn in work properly.
4. Clean-up your materials.
5. Help with group clean-up.
6. Wait to be excused.
7. Push in your chair quietly.
8. Move quietly to the next task.

WORKING

1. Start when signaled to begin.
2. Follow directions.
3. Use time wisely.
4. Strive for your personal best.
5. Ask for help as needed.
6. Help others when it is appropriate.
7. Work quietly and stay on task.
8. Share supplies with group members

Figure 2.2—Student Responsibilities in Small Groups

Communicate Effectively

We think of communication at school as the way we speak, talk with students, listen to them and give directions. However, basic communication skills are as much about attitude and managing student interactions as about speaking and listening. To develop effective communication in small groups, ask yourself:

How will I start my activity?
What types of praise do I give to students?
What signals and techniques encourage students to listen and participate?
How do students know when to start the activity?
How do students get permission to leave my group?
Do I encourage "I" statements?

How will I start my activity?

Managing a small group includes establishing a safe, friendly atmosphere where academic risks are encouraged. Distractions are minimized by meeting in a location where the focus rests on the students. And you, the adult assistant, understand how to manage the group.

To begin an activity, plan what you will say. Include a greeting to the students and a brief overview of the day's task.

Example:

"Welcome to the current events group. Today we are reading about earthquakes around the world."

Go over any pertinent small group expectations. Don't rush your introduction, but move to the activity as soon as possible.

Example:

"Remember that in this group we will read silently and then discuss what we read. We will actively listen to each other when we share our personal experiences with earthquakes."

Active listening is a key in small groups. Assistants need to model eye contact, appropriate body language and tone of voice. You must explain to the students the importance of looking at the person who is speaking while sitting still.

The speaker understands there will be no interrupted as long as comments are concise and on topic. Even if others do not agree, the speaker will be respected.

Young students have difficulty being still. For their groups, limit student speaking to one or two sentences. Then ask a pertinent follow-up question or restate the person's remarks to demonstrate active listening.

Example:

"When I call on you, I want you to tell us one thing that happened last week during the earthquake. Practice your one sentence in your head, then raise your thumb when you are ready to share."

With modeling and practice, students learn to listen with the intent of asking their own pertinent question or adding information. Each has a chance to share their thinking, experiences and questions during the activity.

Examples:

"Mary noticed the lights swaying during the quake? Did anyone else? (Wait for nods.) Tell us what else you observed."

Students become excited when a discussion begins. If their conversation slides off the topic, stop them and refocus their comments to the current discussion.

Example:

"Mary, I know you want to tell us about your aunt's new cat, but right now we're talking about the earthquake. Did the cat run and hide during the quake?"

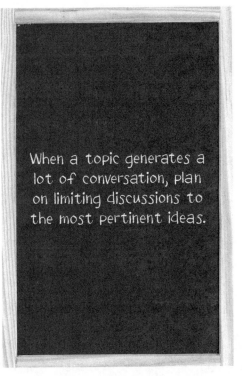

When a topic generates a lot of conversation, plan on limiting discussions to the most pertinent ideas.

When a topic generates a lot of conversation, plan on limiting discussions to the most pertinent ideas. Use drawings, individual student writing, and paired discussions when time allows.

Example:

"I know you have many things to tell us about the earthquake. For the next few minutes we'll be drawing and writing in a booklet called The Day We Had the Earthquake. Think about what you want us to know. Draw what you remember. Add sound words to help us understand your experience."

Have your materials organized and ready to hand out, remembering to keep back the "key item" until the directions are completed. In the case of the earthquake, if you are planning to draw and write in the booklets, withhold the drawing materials.

What types of praise do I give to students?

The following "words of praise" are commonly used.

wonderful   *excellent*

well done   *I'm proud of you*

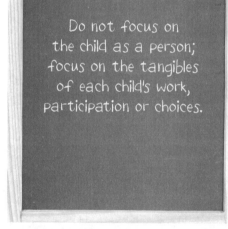

Praise is Tricky.

Do not focus on the child as a person; focus on the tangibles of each child's work, participation or choices.

These represent your opinion and are subjective, vague or off-target. Instead, we want students to evaluate their own work whenever possible. The Shift from Subjective to Objective Statements chart, at the end of this chapter, will provide suggestions.

When you tell students they've done a marvelous job and inside their heads they think their efforts were only so-so, it confuses them. Since we can't see inside students and know what they are thinking, it's important to remain objective.

Praise is tricky. Do not focus on the child as a person; focus on the tangibles of each child's work, participation or choices. Remind them of the goals for the activity, the quality of work, the group's action, the quality of their thought, or the positive direction their work is headed. Speak in a respectful tone of voice.

Examples:

"Your sentence is well-organized and shares interesting information, James."

"Mary, your math equations and your words show your thinking."

"Tim, that's an important idea. Include that in your report."

"You've presented your ideas in sequential order."

Students are accustomed to subjective praise, so the change will confuse them. But, when you evaluate their work objectively, you encourage them to evaluate themselves against their own skills.

Example:

Mary asked, "Do you like the way I did my fish drawing?" Typical answer: "It's very nice." Better answers: "What do you like about what you drew?" or, "I see you have included sea plants. Tell me about the drawing."

What signals and techniques encourage students to listen and participate?

Before meeting with a group, select an age-appropriate technique for calling on students that maintains order and involves everyone. Consider the following quiet signals. We have provided them on a chart at the end of this chapter and downloadable from www.PaddyEger.com:

1. Eyes on the leader

2. Give me "5"

3. Thumb up

4. Passing a small object

5. Whisper to your neighbor

6. Double share

7. 3x5 cards

8. Give advanced notice to reluctant or shy students

9. Show Me

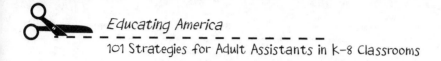
Following are details about each signal or technique. Having a variety of ideas is helpful.

1. Eyes on the leader.

"When I can see everyone's eyes, I will start to call on you. If you have an answer ready, you can blink or wink." This is appropriate for young students.

2. Give Me "5."

Asking young students to "give you 5" means that you expect each one to (1) look at you, (2) quiet their voices (3) quiet their hands, (4) quiet their feet and (5) engage their thinking. When all students comply, begin giving directions, clarifying information and/or calling on students to participate.

3. Thumb up.

Raising hands is not the best way to request answers in a small group. Once a few hands are raised, students who feel unsure shutdown ("Whew! I'm off the hook!"). Instead, say, "When you have an idea about how we can solve this problem, raise your thumb in front of you."

Thumb up is a small motion. One thumb is quietly raised in front of the student's own chest or pointed up from their hand resting on the table. This motion doesn't distract students who are still thinking about an answer.

If you use 'wait time' and delay taking answers for an extra 5 to 10 seconds, you reduce the pressure to perform that instant. More students have time to think of an answer during the quiet moment 'wait time' creates. This technique is appropriate for all ages. Wait time is discussed later and in the glossary.

4. Passing a small object.

Select a small squishy ball, a pocket-size stuffed animal or a roll of tape. Have a student hold the object while speaking. Only that person may speak.

All eyes are expected to be focused on the speaker. After speaking, the object is handed, not tossed, to another person. This is appropriate for all ages.

5. Whisper to your neighbor.

Students listen to a question and respond after consulting with the student seated next to them in a whisper.

Example:

"Whisper to your neighbor what 3+3 equals. If you both agree, each of you put a thumb up."

When students collaborate, there is time for each to hear the other person's ideas. Getting assistance from a peer rather than an adult often proves more comfortable for students. This is appropriate for all ages. Be warned, when little kids whisper their breathiness may tickle your ear.

6. Double share.

If you have an uneven number of students, ask the students to whisper to the person on either side. If their answers agree, each student raises a thumb. This allows instant involvement and students stay focused.

When a student is unsure of an appropriate there is the chance to hear at least one good response. This increases all students' ability to respond appropriately. Use this technique with all ages.

7. 3x5 cards.

In an effort to include all students, put each student name on a 3x5 card. Shuffle the cards for the group and explain that you will call on the name that appears on the top card. Once a student is called on, that name goes to the bottom of the stack.

When you reach the first name again, announce you are reshuffling the cards to create a new, random order. If students know you're using a random order, they will need to pay close attention. The wildly waving hands are quieted and you have better control of the group.

For an even greater random order, put the name of the student who just answered *in* the stack instead of at the bottom. Let the students know what you have done. Tell them that some students will get extra turns that day. Strive to give each student at least one turn during a task.

8. Give advanced notice to reluctant or shy students.

Let reluctant and shy students know when you will call on them. Say the student name *before* asking the question. Even a brief warning helps students refocus and be ready to answer.

Examples:

"Mary, the next question is saved for you."

"Pat, be ready; I'll call on you very soon."

While we want all students to participate, we do not want to make students uncomfortable or pressured so they will not join in. Go slow with reluctant or shy students. Give them an early turn with easier questions.

9. Show Me.

Start by saying, "Show me your thumb if you know what 3+3 equals." An even stronger approach is to ask an open question.

Example:

"How many different ways can you make '6'?"

An open question allows multiple answers: 15-9, 36 ÷6, 100-94, etc. Answers can go on forever! It stimulates the group to reach greater depth in thinking. The excitement becomes electric and allows all students to participate equally, regardless of their understanding of '6.'

How do students know when to start the activity?

It is best to begin a group session with a clear work area, keeping all pertinent materials out of sight beside you on the floor or at least out of reach. Students often come to groups with their own expectations of what they will be doing. If you want to be in control, have them listen to the directions before they "take off" on the task.

Watch groups of people, any age, seated at a table where materials are readily available. Whatever is on the table, within reach, ends up in their hands. Taking materials away isn't as effective as never having them available. So keep the group focused by controlling materials.

Organize your directions. Take time to check that all students have the same information and know the expectations for the task. If some students need more details, start the group on the task then assist them.

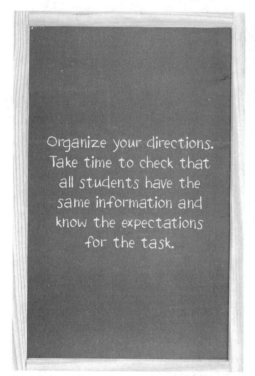

Organize your directions. Take time to check that all students have the same information and know the expectations for the task.

Students are always ready to start before they know what to do. A prepared group leader will have planned how to introduce the activity in a brief meaningful way. And, at the very least, will have kept the pencils and paper or the "key items" under control until the last direction is given.

Example:

"As soon as you have a pencil, put your name on the top and number to seven down the left side of the paper. When I see every pencil resting back down on the table, I'll know you are ready to hear the first question."

How do students get permission to leave my group?

As the adult leader, you must know the whereabouts of all students in your group at all times. This is a safety issue as well as an important part of group control. Understand and use the classroom plan for students who are leaving the group to go anywhere. If the classroom has no plan, suggest that a plan be instituted.

Keep a special note pad or notebook to write down who left, when (date and time), where they went and when they returned.

Whether a student is going to the rest room, working with a specialist, leaving for an appointment or getting a drink, keep track of the student's location. When the school has a fire safety or other emergency drill, teachers must account for all students. You are expected to know the location of all the students in your group. Keeping track of students on a daily basis is easier than suddenly trying to remember where a student has gone.

Do not allow students to leave your group while you give directions. It is both a courtesy and a necessity for them to hear directions and know your expectations. After directions is a more appropriate time for getting drinks, going to the rest room or getting their supplies. Better still, ask them to do those activities during a classroom break time.

If a student chronically leaves your group, that may be a sign of stress, trying to escape a task or a bad habit. Share your observations with the teacher who may not be aware of that student's behavior.

Who left	When (date / time)	To where	Returned.
James	3/2-9:45	speach	10:15
Milly	3/2 10:30	Nurse	—
Bill	3/7 8:30	tutor	9:30
Mary	3/7 10:00	home	—
Jeff	3/15 9:45	testing	10:30
Tom	3/20 11:15	pictures	11:30

Do I encourage "I" statements?

"I" statements tell others how their present behavior makes you feel. They convey your message without finger-pointing or anger and without making people feel un-liked by the speaker.

"I" statements are appropriate for adults as well as students. A non-judgmental patterned sentence is spoken: "When you _____ it makes me feel _____."

Examples:

"When you don't help us clean up our supplies, it makes me feel unhappy that we will need to spend more time cleaning and will miss out on playing a game."

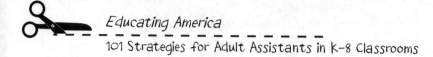

"When you talk during work time it makes me feel frustrated because I can't get my work done."

Using "I" statements takes time, practice and a point of view that most adults as well as children are not accustomed to using. The shift from subjective to objective statements communicates our wishes rather than our complaints.

When students ask questions, decide if their real request stems from lack of information, confusion, starting an overwhelming task, need for reassurance or tiredness. Encourage them to feel free to express themselves. Providing a safe, nurturing environment goes a long way to helping students understand how they learn and how to express their concerns.

Signals and Techniques to Encourage Student Participation

- Eyes on the leader

- Give me "5"

- Thumb up

- Passing a small object

- Whisper to your neighbor

- Double share

- 3x5 cards

- Give advanced notice to reluctant or shy learners

- Show Me

Figure 3.1—Signals and Techniques to Encourage Student Participation

Shift from Subjective to Objective Statements.

When you think...	Say this instead:
"You sure made a mess!"	"I need help picking up our supplies."
"Don't pester me!"	"I need you to wait just a minute before I can help you."
"You should know THAT!"	"I know you can figure this out."
"Shame on you!"	"I feel upset when I see you mistreat our books and supplies."

Students often communicate more than words say
Whenever possible, help students feel free to express themselves.

When a child says...	Answer:
"I don't know how..."	"Do the best you can." "What do you think you are to do?
"How do you spell..."	"Use your best invented spelling."
"What does this say...?"	"What are you trying to say?" "What sounds do you hear?"
"Can you read this?"	"Read it to me; I'll listen." I'll listen as you read this to me."
"Do you like my picture?"	"Tell me about your picture." "What do you like about it?" "I see you have shown..."
"I don't want to do this (varied responses) anymore."	"Show me what you've done so far."

Figure 3.2—Shift from Subjective to Objective Statements

Expand Questioning Strategies

Asking and answering questions is a skill students need to develop. While 'yes-no' answers are useful, they are the weakest form of answer. Open-ended questions and other strategies encourage students to share their deeper thinking skills. See Questioning Strategies chart at the end of this chapter or visit www.PaddyEger.com. Remember to:

Ask clear, concise questions.
Avoid repeating or restating questions or answers.
Implement think-pair-share.
Use wait time.
Ask follow-up questions.
Brainstorm.
Use a variety of questioning techniques.

Ask clear, concise questions.

Encourage students to restate the essence of the question they answer and speak in complete sentences.

Example:

"Name four landforms near your home."

Answer: "Lake, river, hill and valley"

Better answer: "Four landforms near my home are a lake, a river, a hill and a valley."

Best answer: "Four landforms near my home are Lake Emerson, the Colorado River, Becker's Hill and Maple Valley."

Avoid repeating or restating questions or answers.

Students will not practice active listening if you do the listening for them. When you hear yourself repeating questions, revise the way you ask them. Be more concise. Preface questions by saying, "The first question is…" Pause until all students are focused on you, then finish the sentence.

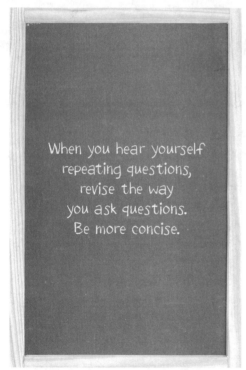

When you hear yourself repeating questions, revise the way you ask questions. Be more concise.

Example:

"The first question is…what is a landform?"

Some students need coaching on how to listen. Ask them to repeat what they thought they heard you say. If a student is still confused, ask another student to rephrase the question. Then go back to the first student to repeat what was heard.

Example:

"What four landforms are near your home?"

Anna: "What do you mean?"

Assistant: "What do you think you heard me say?"

Anna: "Something about stuff near my home."

Assistant: "That's right. Mary, repeat the question for Anna."

Mary: "We need to name four landforms near our houses, like Lake Emerson."

Assistant: "Anna, what did Mary tell you?"

Anna: "I'm naming four places near my house like Lake Emerson."

Implement think-pair-share.

Partner students to share their thinking. This provides a opportunity to mix strong students with those less sure of themselves.

Ask one question for all pairs to answer. Limit the time for the pairs to talk together (2-5 minutes). When the time ends, ask each to share their answers. The pairs can write their answers and/or share them aloud. After all the answers have been presented, discuss them. Use their ideas to generate more questions or proceed to the next part of the task.

Think-Pair-Share

Partner students to share their thinking.

Mix stronger students with those less sure of themselves.

Example:

"Which words from the story best describe the main character?" After hearing all answers ask: "How are the words on our list similar or different?" This will stimulate discussion.

Use wait time.

If the question is important enough to ask, it is important enough to wait for thoughtful answers. During the silence, students search for their best answer, not just the first one that pops up. Remember to wait up to ten seconds before assisting a student by rephrasing the question or asking if the student wants help from another student.

Use wait time:

If the question is important enough to ask, it is important enough to wait for thoughtful answers.

Example:

"Today I want you to think of four landforms near your home. Try to think of their names and when you have been there. When you are ready, raise your thumb on the table."

Wait time encourages students to dig deeper to find their best responses. When you add more details for them to consider you need to increase wait time. Remember to praise their efforts.

Example:

"Mary asked you to explain how the three children worked together to solve their problems. She asked you a thinking question that has many possible answers rather than asking you to tell one way the problem was solved."

Call on students randomly or use your 3x5 name cards. Remember to give shy or reluctant students time to prepare before asking them questions. If you use 3x5 cards, remember to shuffle them each time you return to the first name.

Ask follow-up questions.

Follow-up questions encourage students to be active listeners during discussion.

Example:

"Mary, do you agree with Anna?"

Mary: "What?"

Assistant: "Anna, repeat what you just said."

Anna: "I said, I think the three children were smart to ask Mrs. Frill to help them plan what to say to Mr. Billy."

Assistant: "Mary, do you agree with Anna?"

For math, science, and process questions, encourage students to share how they arrived at their answer.

Example:

"Mary, use the whiteboard and show us how you added such a long list of numbers."

Thinking and questioning techniques form an unending list. Remember to use a variety of strategies.

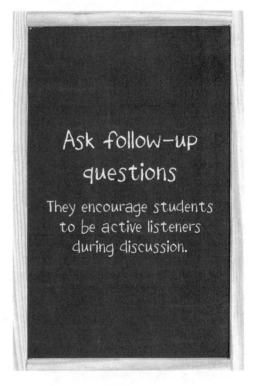

Ask follow-up questions

They encourage students to be active listeners during discussion.

Brainstorm.

Brainstorming is the process of letting thoughts flow without judging their importance or accuracy. Students create lists of information and questions about a topic. All students, regard-

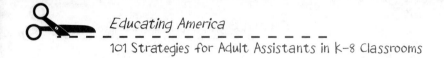

less of background knowledge or level of thinking skills, can participate.

A few rules are needed for effective brainstorming.

1. Select a question or topic.

2. Use a whiteboard or large paper for recording student questions and answers. Older students can select a note taker to write down ideas and a moderator to call on students to speak. Dividing tasks keeps the students involved and the activity moving.

3. Call on students in an orderly manner such as thumb up or pass the object.

4. Accept all ideas and answers. This includes funny, unimportant and outrageous ideas.

5. Work for *quantity*. Go beyond the easy ideas. Use wait time, allowing students to sift through their brains for more detailed information. Accept answers as long as the students keep unpacking more and more ideas. Once focus lags, move on.

6. Encourage students to "hitchhike" or piggyback off each other's ideas.

Brainstorming in a small or large group often begins with open-ended questions. The activity will consume most of a period and needs to be part of the goal in the current or up-coming task.

Examples:

"Can you think of words that mean almost the same as 'run'?"

"How many ways can you make 25?"

"What sports use a ball?"

"Who are America's heroes?"

Another way to brainstorm is to record student information in a 3-column chart:
What do I know?
What do I want to know?
What questions do I still have?

Example:

"We are going to begin a study of rocks. First, let's see what we already know about rocks."

Use a blank sheet of paper. Divide it into three columns. For the study on rocks write one question at the top of each column:

"What do I already know about rocks?"

"What do I want to know about rocks?"

"What questions do I still have about rocks?" (Use after the task is finished)

What do I already know about rocks?	What do I want to know about rocks?	What questions do I still have about rocks?

Write student responses, unedited, under the first two questions. This is brainstorming at its best. Students feed off other's comments, allowing you to record more and more information.

As you record student answers, misunderstandings, "holes" in their learning and their interests in the topic become clear. This gives you a starting place to review their knowledge and begin building new information. Do not expect to answer every question on their brainstorming list.

When a unit of study ends, brainstorm again to check new understandings. Go back to the original list. Read through their earlier statements. Correct errors using a different colored pen. Enjoy a laugh with them over their mistakes or misunderstandings.

Talk about what they have learned and the questions that remain unanswered. Praise what they've learned and challenge them to think up new questions. Write their new questions in the third column. These questions can be answered through individual research projects or kept for future use.

Brainstorming is an engaging cooperative, energy-charged activity. Once you've tried it, you'll want to use it often. But, don't overdo it; the power and energy it creates may fade with overuse.

Use a variety of questioning techniques.

Benjamin Bloom created the following classifications of questions based on his six levels of cognitive learning. His levels include:

- *Recall*
- *Comprehension*
- *Application*
- *Analysis*
- *Synthesis*
- *Evaluation*

Let's assume the students read a book about a boy who lived with his family in a cabin in the woods for twelve years. Recently he went to live in a large city in a mansion with relatives he's never met.

Below are questions related to Bloom's classifications. The depth of thinking required for answering the questions increases as you move through the list. This chart is available at the end of this chapter and downloadable from www.PaddyEger.com.

🍎 *Recall* questions often begin with: who, what, when, where, how. They depend on the learner remembering details from the reading or discussions.

Examples:

"Who is the main character in the story?"

"Where does the story take place?"

🍎 *Comprehension* questions ask for organization and selecting appropriate details, facts or ideas. They begin with the words: retell, summarize, restate.

Examples:

"Tell us about the main character's eating habits."

"Summarize the boy's adventures from the woods to the mansion."

Ask students to restate the information in their own words. They can use ideas from the text, but must share them in conversational language, not in the 'book speak' language of the authors. Short quotes may be included but must be presented as quotes from the text.

Examples:

"Write the main idea of this chapter in 1, 2 or 3 sentences in your own words."

Recall questions often begin with: who, what, when, where, how.

Comprehension questions ask for organization and selecting appropriate details, facts or ideas.

"The early explorers landed in several locations along the east coast of the Americas. Look at the map and decide why they chose the woods where Sam lived as one of their favorite places to camp."

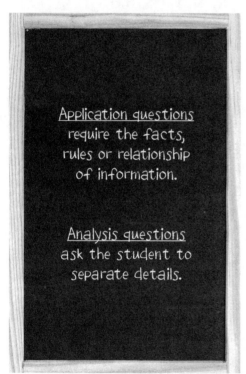

Application questions require the facts, rules or relationship of information.

Analysis questions ask the student to separate details.

🍎 *Application* questions require the facts, rules or relationship of information. They begin with the words: How is... like...? Why is...significant?

Examples:

"How do Sam's eating habits change?"

"Why is Sam's old blanket significant?"

🍎 *Analysis* questions ask the student to separate details. Questions begin with the words: classify, compare and contrast, outline.

Examples:

"Compare Sam's feelings about his old home to his new home."

"Outline the steps Sam used to learn table manners."

🍎 *Synthesis* questions require students to elaborate, or combine new information with previous knowledge. Questions ask: "What do you predict..., What ideas might you add...?, What solutions would you suggest...?"

Examples:

"How can the step-family help Sam feel more comfortable at meal time?"

"What do you predict might happen if Sam moved back to the woods?"

🍎 *Evaluation* questions ask the student to make judgments and state opinions. They begin with phrases like: Do you agree that...? What do you think about...? What was the most important..?

Examples:

"Sam felt discouraged when he first moved in with the new family. Which things he tried worked the best? Why do you think that is so?"

"What do you think about the nosy neighbor next to the mansion calling the police?"

Taking a survey is another way to evaluate student thinking. Use 'thumb up' for a quick survey. When a group has strong feelings, encourage them to explain how they feel and why. You may extend it further and ask students to write their opinions.

Examples:

"Raise your thumb if you feel Sam needs to control his temper."

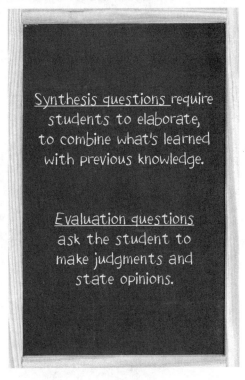

Synthesis questions require students to elaborate, to combine what's learned with previous knowledge.

Evaluation questions ask the student to make judgments and state opinions.

"Why do you think that Sam got so angry when his new family criticized his eating habits? What would you do if you were Sam?"

Discussions and written answers include more students than a simple one-step survey such as "raise your thumb." Sharing information energizes the task and engages student thinking.

Questioning Strategies

- Ask clear, concise questions

- Do not repeat or restate questions or answers

- Think-Pair-Share

- Use wait time

- Praise student attempts to ask thoughtful questions

- Call on students randomly or use your 3x5 name cards.

- Ask follow-up questions

- Brainstorm

- Use a variety of questioning techniques

Figure 4.1—Questioning Strategies

Bloom's Questioning Techniques

Bloom established a hierarchy of questioning strategies.
Work with students to develop their answering techniques.

Recall–
  Remember details from reading, discussion or an activity.
  Use the vocabulary: who, what, when, where, how.

Comprehension –
  Select appropriate details.
  Use the vocabulary: retell, summarize, restate.

Application–
  Begin to see relationships.
  Use the vocabulary: How is __ like __?
  Why is __ significant?

Synthesis–
  Elaborate or combine ideas to create something new.
  Use the vocabulary: predict, suggest.

Evaluation–
  Make judgments and state opinions.
  Use the vocabulary: Do you agree?
  Why is ____ important?

Figure 4.2—Bloom's Questioning Techniques

Deal with Misbehavior

Misbehavior/discipline problems can be scary. Classroom assistants often comment, "What if the students don't listen?", "What if they won't do what I ask them to do?" or "It just isn't the same as dealing with my own children."

Student misbehavior exists for several reasons. The more common reasons include:

🍎 Personal issues: hunger, sickness, abuse, anger, or the desire for attention

🍎 Uncertainty about group expectations and/or how to fit into the group

🍎 Inability to understand the task

🍎 Inconsistent, ill-prepared or off-task adult assistants

Most students want and expect you to take charge of their small groups and provide a sense of security and continuity for them. Occasionally, students want to take control of the group to gain attention or may attempt to keep the group off-task to avoid starting the task.

To maintain your role as group leader, use the Ways to Focus Your Group Chart at the end of this chapter. This chart may be downloaded from www.PaddyEger.com

When you plan the activity and think through your expectations, there is a greater probability that the group will stay on track. Work through these suggestions as you start to plan.

Come to the group prepared to lead the task.

State the goals of the task clearly.

Set clear expectations and limits then stick to them.
Create an action plan for disruptive students.
Compliment desired behavior and quality work.
Use rewards sparingly.
Keep the group activity focused.

Respect student answers.
Monitor student progress and adjust to individual needs.
Keep track of your allotted time.
End all groups with positive actions.
Update the teacher on activity and student performance outcomes.

Come to the group prepared to lead the task.

Come to the group prepared to lead the task.

Know the goal of the activity and how you will begin the task. Will you start with a hook activity, a brief review, introduce a new task, or start right to work? Do you have the needed materials gathered and ready for use? Have you planned your introduction so it will engage the students? What important tool or supporting material will you hold back to focus student attention until you finish giving the directions?

State the goals of the task clearly.

Explain the activity in a simple sentence.

Example:

"Today we will talk about and practice eight math spelling words to prepare for writing math observations next week."

Explain how a new activity relates to another skill they already know.

Example:

"Let's take the math problem 3x3 apart. Multiplication is a pattern for adding numbers in groups. 3x3 is 3+3+3 or 3 groups of 3. When we work through the math, both equal the same amount."

Set clear expectations and limits then stick to them.

Use expectations that match both teacher and school goals. Review the expectations through compliments made to students or by having students model the skills.

Use expectations that match both teacher and school goals.

Examples:

"Thank you for coming quietly to our group."

"Remember how we sit to share the table space?"

"Show me how I will know you are ready to listen?"

Create an action plan for disruptive students.

The best way to handle disruptive students is to follow the classroom teacher's lead. Watch the teacher. Listen to the phrases used. Notice how the teacher physically moves around the room, and monitors for off-task or unacceptable behavior while keeping the rest of the class focused on the discussion or directions.

Misbehavior also occurs as a group begins a task or moves to a new activity. Watch how the teacher controls transition times. Copy the techniques you see and hear. They are based on the teacher's experience of what works best for the class.

When students slip out of control or disrupt the group, take action quickly. Use the teacher's discipline plan or follow the Misbehavior Four-Step Plan, an escalating system found at the end of this chapter and downloadable from www.PaddyEger.com

A four-step system

Step one:
Give a non-verbal reminder.

Step two:
Talk quietly and privately with the student.

Step three:
Move the disruptive student to another location.

Step four:
Take the student to talk with the teacher.

Step One: Give a non-verbal reminder.

Focus on the disruptive student with a serious look, a gentle touch on the hand or a touch to the edge of a work paper. Simple warnings and/or praise often lead students to modify their behavior.

Examples:

"I like the way James is starting his work without talking."

"Thank you for passing the books carefully. That is very considerate."

Step Two: **Talk quietly and privately with the student.**

Move away from the group for that conversation

Examples:

"Mary, you seem to have a hard time listening today. What can I do to help you become part of our group?"

"Mary, can you tell me why you are not waiting for your turn today?"

Let the student answer. Explain what changes you expect to be made. Discuss the lesson briefly to insure the student can resume work.

Example:

"I need you to use a quieter voice and to share the table space with other students. Do you understand?" (Wait for a response.)

"When you go back to the group, put your name on the top of your paper and begin writing the words in alphabetical order. I'll be watching, and, I'll be ready to help you if I see your thumb raised on the desk."

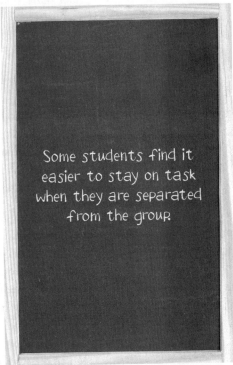

Some students find it easier to stay on task when they are separated from the group

Step Three. Move the disruptive student to another location.

Sometimes a simple shift in seating remedies a situation.

Example:

"I have moved you out of the group so you can focus better. When you are prepared to return to the group and follow our directions, you may rejoin us. This is your last warning. Our next step will be to talk with the teacher."

Some students find it easier to stay on task when they are separated from the group. If possible, have a nearby space available for use after directions are given. Remember to include these students when the review and clean-up are started.

With younger students, a brief change of activity, like a stretch or sending the disruptive student on a brief task (bring a stapler to the group, put away extra papers, etc.) provides a chance for the student to regain self-control without adult intervention.

Step Four: **Take the student to talk with the teacher.**

Stay calm when you reach this step. Explain to the teacher what you observed and the steps you've used with the student.

Example:

"Ms. Smith, Mary needs to speak with you. I spoke privately with her about interrupting. She said she'd remember the rules, but then she continued to shout at children in her group even when she was seated at the extra table. I think she needs to explain her decisions to you."

Your responsibility for the disrupter ends once the teacher begins speaking with the student. Return to your group and continue with the task. Student privacy dictates that discussing the disruptive student with the group, other assistants, or students is not acceptable.

Let the teacher set the course of action or consequences for the disruptive student. That's a teacher responsibility. You will need to work with the off-task student in the future so do not create a negative situation.

When the student returns, start fresh; watch for ways to compliment improved behavior. A sincere smile or a positive comment signals a fresh start.

Asking the teacher to "take over" is not a sign of failure; it indicates that you know you've reached a place where an intervention is needed. However, if problems continue, set up a meeting with the teacher for advice on how to change your style or method of setting expectations and following through.

Do not argue with students. It is counter productive. Listen to their concerns with an open mind. Let them know which expectations they are ignoring or what behavior they are not controlling, but do not argue with them. They will outlast any argument you initiate. Also, the rest of the group will suffer from your lack of attention to their needs.

Begin each day as a "fresh start" for everyone in your group. It signals that you are fair, forgiving and reasonable.

Compliment desired behavior and quality work.

Stop the group after the first five minutes of work to check their progress. Use that time to compliment specific student effort on a skill.

Show acceptance, sincerity, and understanding in your tone, facial expression, body language and posture.

Examples:

"I appreciate the quiet work time this group is providing each other."

"Wow! You all remembered to put your name on your paper!"

"Thank you for taking turns and sharing your ideas. We have twenty minutes left to work today so let's get back to our reading."

Show acceptance, sincerity, and understanding in your tone, facial expression, body language and posture. Look students in the eye as you acknowledge their answers. If some students wish to share their beginning ideas, encourage them to share then send the group back to the task.

Use rewards sparingly.

If the group has problems settling down, a reward might be helpful. Consult the teacher. You need to stay within the classroom guidelines.

Start with a verbal reward. Know that immature groups may need a more tangible reward: stickers, a chance to play a favorite game, or points toward a special activity.

Examples:

"Thank you for using all your skills today. We finished right on time."

"Today everyone listened, took turns and worked quietly. Let's spend time working on the covers of our science notebooks."

Extrinsic prizes like candy, toys and trinkets need to be avoided. Learning should be the prize. Plus, extrinsics may cause disappointment for students who are not allowed to accept such things. It may also create competition with other assistants who cannot or do not choose to provide prizes.

Keep the group activity focused.

- Pace the activity so there is little time for misbehavior.
- Call on all students equally, not just those who try to answer first.
- Use quiet signals like "thumb up".
- Ask questions that cannot be answered by "yes" or "no." Start with:
  "Tell me..."   "Show the largest..."   "Describe..."
  "How many ways can you...?"   "Compare..."

🍎 Use wait time. It allows students extra time to think of their best answers.

Respect student answers.

When students have problems answering questions, help them handle their misinformation and wrong answers so they will not feel embarrassed in the group

Example

"How are 3, 6, 9 and 12 related?"
Mary: "3 plus 6 is 9."

Provide a hint to Mary without telling her the answer. In this instance rephrase or restate the question yourself.

Example:

"Mary, you added 3 and 6. They do equal 9. Now look at the bigger pattern. Can you see how 3, 6, 9 and 12 make a pattern if we keep them in order?"

Allow Mary time to think. If the group becomes restless, offer a challenge:

Example:

"While I help Mary, I want the rest of you to write down the numbers that would appear next if the pattern continued on six more numbers."

While they work, help Mary follow the pattern and understand that each following number increases by '3'.

Ask Questions that Start with:

- "Tell me..."
- "Show the largest..."
- "Describe..."
- "How many ways can you...?"
- "Compare..."

Monitor student progress and adjust to individual needs.

Pace the task to match the skill level of the group. If you want quality work, provide adequate quiet work time and support for all students.

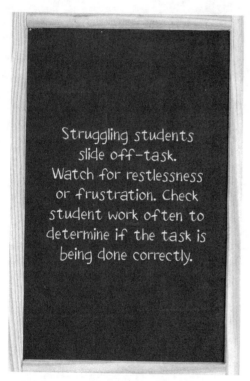

Struggling students slide off-task. Watch for restlessness or frustration. Check student work often to determine if the task is being done correctly.

Know when to stop talking. Keep student chatter and your interruptions to a minimum. Model quietness; whisper with students who need your assistance. When a group has an extended quiet time, students have a greater opportunity to produce quality work.

Struggling students may slide off-task. Watch for restlessness or frustration. Check their work often to determine if the task is being done correctly. If not, talk with them, explaining what changes are needed.

Expecting a student to rework everything from the beginning is overwhelming and may cause a student to give up or refuse to go back and make the changes. Instead, circle the item numbers that need to be checked. After discussing one or two of the problems, draw a line across the paper and begin any necessary changes below the line. The student can go back and makes changes above the line after completing the task below the line.

If a task is sequenced, use your discretion about what and how much needs to be completed. Work for understanding the activity rather than finishing everything.

Stay alert to student reactions over the changed task. Not completing everything may frustrate some students. You will need to decide how to handle it based on your individual situation. Remember to check back with the student every few minutes and give a 5-minute reminder at the end.

Example:

"I see everyone is working carefully. Today please stop after you finish your next sentence. We will complete this task the next time we meet."

When students get off-track, direct them back to the task by focusing on a specific detail of their work to "reconsider," share, change, or restate.

Examples:

"What does this word (pointing to word) mean?"

"I see you used the word 'sprint' instead of 'run.' Tell us way you chose that word."

"What do you plan to do on the next part of the activity?"

"Remember, we are drawing trees for all four seasons."

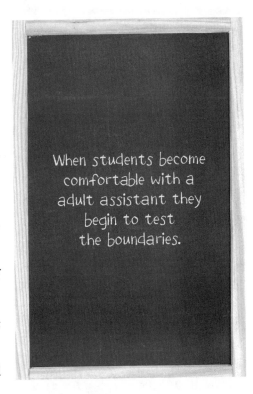

When students become comfortable with a adult assistant they begin to test the boundaries.

When students become comfortable with adult assistants they begin to test your boundaries. Don't accept rude or disrespectful behavior toward yourself or others. Remind them of the teacher's behavior plan or use the Misbehavior Four-Step Plan to settle them.

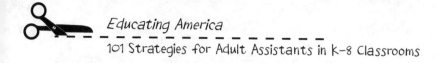
Keep track of your allotted time.

Give a 5-minute warning so students can select an appropriate stopping place. Plan enough time for students to complete an orderly clean-up. Keep the clean up calm and student voice levels low. Remember, uncontrolled transitions and clean-ups lead to noisy and off-task behavior. Plan ahead.

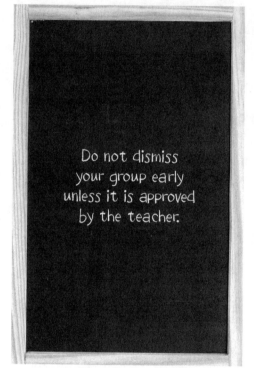

Do not dismiss your group early unless it is approved by the teacher.

Keep an activity in your pocket to fill in unstructured time with students if you complete your task early. Do not dismiss your group early unless that is approved by the teacher. Movement in one group disrupts other groups still working. Respect other group work times by controlling your group's movement.

End all groups with positive actions.

Even if your time with the students was difficult, let them know you like them and appreciate their efforts.

Example:

"Today we got a good start on the math page. Thank you for working quietly and letting others finish as much as possible."

If necessary, explain which behaviors were not acceptable and what changes you expect the next time you meet.

Examples:

"Today this group had a hard time getting started and no one finished. Next time, we will work with quieter voices so you will be able to finish on time."

"Time to go. I'll watch you as you move to...If you are able to do it quietly, I'll mark down 2 points and we'll be closer to our science game activity."

If you say you'll watch them, be certain you do. One or more students will look back.

At your next meeting, hold the group accountable. Remind them of their previous problem and explain your expectations. Watch for their compliance so you can compliment any improvements.

Examples:

"Last week we had difficulty getting down to work. Today, after I give directions, I expect you to start the math puzzle without any reminders."

"Today we need to finish the math puzzle first. I'll come around and help you individually if you have questions. So, turn on your thinking and begin working quietly."

Update the teacher on activity and student performance outcomes.

Record your comments on the teacher's accountability form, in the adult assistant notebook or wherever and however the teacher designates. Begin by relating the successes, positive outcomes and students who formed new understandings. Next, explain student problems. Use the teacher's evaluation form or the Group Evaluation Form sample found at the end of the chapter and downloadable at www.PaddyEger.com.

Other Behavior Considerations

Respect

When the classroom rules don't come to mind, most every behavior can be covered by a blanket of respect.

Respect yourself

Respect others

Respect property

Respect your environment

If a student doesn't finish work, that's lack of self-respect. When a student is noisy and disruptive, that's lack of respect for others. When students don't help clean-up, that's lack of respect for others, school property and the school environment. Add a fifth "R," responsibility, and most group expectations are covered.

How will students treat each other?

All individuals, children and adults, deserve respect. Classroom assistants are role models and must:

Give students full attention when they speak.

Keep eye contact with students when they/you speak.

Respect student answers.

Compliment the quality of individual student work.

How will I help students handle their own problems?

One of the purposes of education is to help students become independent enough to handle their own situations. It is an important goal that can be taught through modeling and practice. Don't rush in to "save" students. We need to encourage them to solve issues through problem-solving techniques, school rules and classroom expectations along with the positive interaction skills they brought from home.

Academic problems are usually best handled by asking a student to go back and think through what needs to be done. When a student says, "I don't get it.", don't start from the beginning. Ask, "What do you think you need to do?" or "What do you remember about what we are working on today?"

Often a student has a small question like "Where do I put my name?" or "Can I do this on my own paper?" If you jump in and give all the directions over again, you may be wasting time. One thing is for sure; you will forget this trick at least once, but when it clicks, it will prevent long minutes of frustration for everyone.

With the responsibility back on the student to rethink the directions, you can guide from the place where the confusion began rather than "from the top."

> If you have a detailed task with multiple steps, provide a written copy of the directions.

If you have a detailed task with multiple steps, provide a written copy of the directions. Students can refer to the directions on their own and ask clarifying questions along the way.

If directions must be repeated, it is wise to have a student restate the directions. They speak the same kid language. Listen in to be sure the explanation is accurate and properly sequenced.

75

But it's my child!

One of the more awkward situations occurs when you work in a group with *your* child or a child from your neighborhood. Sometimes that child acts silly, withdraws, or refuses to work. Because you are there for the entire group, you need to find a way to handle the situation tactfully.

In our classroom one parent and child decided to call each other by more formal names; Dad became 'Mr. Smith' and the child became 'Miss Smith.' It sounds silly, but it worked for them while they adjusted to their new roles.

When a behavioral problem arises between your child or a friend's child and another student, encourage the students to solve the problem. Take off your "parent or neighbor hat" if you cannot find a neutral adult to mediate the situation.

One year in our primary classroom, a parent attempted to mediate a recess problem with her own child. The parent of child 'A' got the two children together to discuss the problem. Child 'A' felt her parent was taking sides with child 'B.' Child 'B' didn't think the adult was being fair and was favoring child 'A.' When the discussion ended 5 minutes later, all three were near tears and the problem still dangled in the air.

The wisest choice is to stay out of the middle when you know one of the children. Regardless of who is in-the-right or in-the-wrong, if you stay neutral you can provide 110% support later at school or when the problem comes home to the neighborhood.

Encouraging and supporting students to handle their problems leaves us out of the loop. When children learn to express their concerns in a positive way and begin to talk through their problems, they are developing important life skills.

Ways to Focus Your Group

- Come to the group prepared to lead the task.

- State the goal of the task clearly.

- Set clear expectations and limits then stick to them.

- Use group dynamics to maintain control of the group.

- Create an action plan for disruptive students.

- Compliment desired behavior and quality work.

- Use rewards sparingly.

- Keep the group activity focused.

- Respect student answers.

- Monitor student progress and adjust to support individual needs.

- Keep track of the allotted time.

- End all groups with positive actions.

Figure 5.1—Ways to Focus Your Group

Misbehavior Four-Step Plan

When students misbehave, institute the teacher's
plan or use the following:

Step One:
Give the student a non-verbal reminder:
  A serious look
  A gentle touch on the hand or the edge
  of a work paper

Step Two:
Talk quietly and privately with the student away
from the group.

Step Three:
Move the disruptive student to another
location or ask an on-task person to trade
places with the disrupter.
Keep track of the disrupter.

Step Four:
Take the disrupter to the teacher. Explain the
problem then return to your group.

Remember, when the student returns to your group
give the student a fresh start.

Figure 5.2—Misbehavior Four-Step Plan

Group Evaluation Form

Group _____ Date _____

Activity _____ Adult _____

Today's Successes!

_____
_____
_____
_____
_____

Questions/Concerns

_____
_____
_____
_____
_____

Student level of focus on today's task:
  1   2   3   4   5   6   7   8   9   10 (wonderful!)
  Comments:

_____
_____
_____

Student behavior and cooperation on today's task:
  1   2   3   4   5   6   7   8   9   10 (wonderful!)
  Comments:

_____
_____
_____

Figure 5.3—Group Evaluation Form

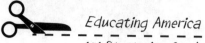

Develop Thinking Skills

Our thinking processes develop as we grow and practice our skills. We can guide students to develop their ability to:

Observe the world through their senses
Communicate what their senses tell them
Compare what they see to other things they know
Organize what they know
Understand relationships
Infer or predict new patterns
Apply knowledge to solve new problems

Observe

Observation depends on using our senses to explain the world. It involves hands-on experiences with sight, sound, touch, smell and taste to explore the features of an object. At school, young observers might match dots to numbers, watch the weather outside the window or find objects that are shades of red. Observation includes spacing printed words, touching a relief globe or studying an illustration for information about a story. These skills come easily to young students as they make direct contact with their physical world.

During observation, encourage students to use descriptive phrases such as: I see…I hear…It feels…I smell…It tastes like…

Examples (in reading groups):

"Can you see two words that start with the letter "b"?"

"As I read, listen for words that rhyme."

"Think about how rain feels on your skin."

"What smells remind you of roses?"

"How would you describe the taste of peppermint candy?"

Begin with these Skills:

Observe

Communicate

Compare organize

Communicate

Communication is the ability to share observations through reading, talking, writing or drawing. It can be done alone, with a partner or with a group. Students develop vocabulary as they explore details and share their thoughts in a meaningful way.

Examples (in reading groups):

"Read the part of the story that tells about the surprise."

"Could you hear how mother felt when she spoke about the lost kitten?"

"Write down action words from the story."

"Draw what you think will happen next in the story."

Compare

Comparison is the skill of finding similarities and differences in two or more objects using your senses as well as size, weight, shape and other measurements. Students view objects, label, manipulate or turn them, estimate their size or weight and test them. They use details to answer questions and make judgments based on their findings.

Comparing items doesn't need to be complicated. Think of oranges and tomatoes: how are they alike? How are they different?

Older students use comparison to explain more complex topics: How is the geography of United States and Togo alike? How is it different?

Examples (in reading groups):

"Tell us which character in the story is most like you and why."

"Locate a repeating or a rhyming pattern in the poem we just read."

"What would have happened if it had rained during the party?"

"Compare how people in India and Ireland celebrate their birthdays."

Use the specific vocabulary for each thinking skill.

Organize

Organization has multiple steps and requires the student to categorize, order, sequence, classify, locate, chart and/or group selected items. When students sift through their background knowledge they refine and classify important information. When they say, "I just did it" they are not sharing their strategy. Students must learn to explain how they organized their thoughts to truly use organizational skills.

The vocabulary for organization includes: describe, explain your thinking, list information or illustrate ideas. Students share ideas through writing, speaking, drawings, acting out information and re-creating scenarios.

Example:

"Tree, bed, shoe, spoon and paper. How are these items alike? Are there any that do not belong? Explain your thinking."

Student 'A' used background experiences and knowledge. "All of these can be made from wood: My bed frame is wooden and my mother's clogs are wooden shoes. I saw native people carving wood so I imagine they make spoons sometimes. And paper is made from wood."

Student 'B' uses auditory (listening) skills then tactile (touch). "All the words but 'paper' have only one syllable. I think paper doesn't belong. Or, maybe tree doesn't belong. I can hold all the things except a tree in my hand."

Student 'C' organizes the information yet another way. "The tree doesn't belong. The rest are things found in a house. I guess there might be a little tree in a house, but we don't have one."

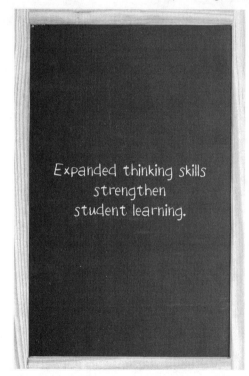

Expanded thinking skills strengthen student learning.

All the students are correct. Discussion begins as they support their own organization while becoming aware of other organizational possibilities.

Organization skills reach into all subject areas. Pose a question. Give the students time to work through their ideas. Spend time sharing answers to the question.

Examples:

Math: "How can you organize the five types of attribute blocks into 3 piles?"

Reading: "List 4 different story genres found in this story collection. Tell us how they are alike and different"

Writing: "Select 4 words to rhyme with 'blame', 'pride' and 'stir'. Use some of the words to create a rhyming poem of six lines."

Science: "List the kinds of weather displayed on the classroom chart last month. Chart our daily weather using easy-to-understand symbols."

Soc. Science: "Classify the types of crops raised in Hawaii and Alaska. Find six crops that could survive in both climates. Explain your choices."

Understand Relationships

As students develop ways to organize information, they begin to observe relationships. They draw on past experiences to create new information, using the attributes of shape, size and pattern to help explain their thinking. When one object or situation reacts or changes, students begin to understand cause and effect.

Encourage students to use key vocabulary words like experiment, survey, discover, rank, question, debate, interpret, question, examine and test when they explain how objects or ideas relate to one another.

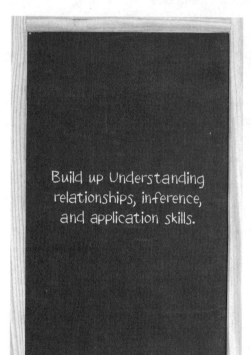

Build up Understanding relationships, inference, and application skills.

Examples:

Math: "Experiment using metric weights. Balance six pairs of unlike objects. Explain your process and findings"

Reading: "Draw a plot line for the story. Examine how the story grows and changes."

Writing/Science combined: "Write about the effects of floods and drought. How are they alike and different?"

Soc. Science: "Examine how bad weather influence crops, rivers and people."

Infer

Inference is the ability to predict outcomes by using past knowledge. New ideas are formulated; learning is transferred. Evaluations are made as old information creates new understandings. Inference uses key words that include: test, generalize, construct, judge, justify, debate, translate, rewrite and theorize.

Try this test with older students. "What is the significance of the letters Q, W, E, R, T, Y, U, I, O, P in this arrangement?" Give ample time for "guessing." Accept all logical answers before sharing their relationship: they form the top row of letters on a computer keyboard.

Examples:

Math: "Jar 'A' has 70 marbles. Estimate the total in jars 'B' and 'C.' Justify your answers."

Reading: "Predict the future of the three main characters."

Writing: "Write a twist and end the story at a point before the author's ending. How does this change the outcome?"

Science: "Use your weather log to predict next week's weather."

Soc. St: "Theorize how native legends relate to real weather."

Apply

Application is the ability to use previous knowledge to solve complex problems. It requires the capacity to adapt, create, invent, design, change, rearrange or imagine differently. It tests the learner's willingness to take educated risks.

Examples:

Math: "Write ten or more ways to make "100" using odd numbers."

Reading: "When do real people make decisions similar to book characters? How do their results compare?"

Writing: "Read two books on various types of pets. Describe how you would select a pet for your best friend's family."

Science: "What three household tools could be adapted for predicting weather? Explain your choices and their uses."

Soc. St: "Select cultures from four continents. How do these diverse people use the golden rule to solve problems"

Develop Thinking Skills

- Multiple answers allow more students to actively participate.

- Thinking out loud encourages others to stay tuned in.

- Unstructured wait time creates enhanced discussions.

- Creative answers emerge; less important data drops away.

- Risk-taking increases.

- Students, not adults "drive" the discussion.

- Misbehavior decreases because students are actively involved.

- Students stay focused longer.

- Unusual questions and ideas surface and are treated with respect.

- Increased discussion stimulates subject-specific vocabulary.

- Curiosity and interest in the topic increases.

Figure 6.1—Develop Thinking Skills

Monitor Student Progress

As students work, we need to monitor the way they perform tasks and use their allotted time. This is one of the busiest times. In light of this, ask yourself the following questions:

What are my work expectations?
How will I introduce new materials?
How much of the task needs to be completed each day?
Does the allotted time match the group needs?
How can students self-monitor their work?
How will I handle off-task behavior?
How will I accommodate students who finish early?
How do I assist slower students and keep them independent?

What are my work expectations?

Tell students 'up front' what you're expecting from them so there are no surprises. Avoid explaining every detail in one conversation. This sounds contradictory. It is. Too little information leaves students without direction. They will interpret the task as they 'think' it should be done.

Example:

"Today we're going to look at maps then draw one."

Too much information weighs down your introduction and may overwhelm students causing many to shutdown.

Example:

"Today we will look and maps and see how colors are used. Then we'll draw our own imaginary island using colors that match the ones we seen. You will need to show a harbor, mountains, a river and a lake. Of course you can add your own touches, but that will come later."

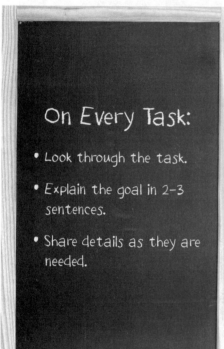

On Every Task:

• Look through the task.

• Explain the goal in 2-3 sentences.

• Share details as they are needed.

So what's the balance? Each task is different. You will need to:

🍎 Look through the task.

🍎 Explain the goal in 2-3 sentences.

🍎 Share details as they are needed.

Example:

"Today we will look at maps to see how colors are used. Then each of you will draw a map of an imaginary island. I'll give you the details when we are ready to start drawing."

There is an exception to releasing details in small bits as a task unfolds. Teachers often create a rubric, a detailed, written plan used for larger projects. It lays out each task with specific directions and requirements that build to the finished project. Rubrics include:

🍎 Overview of the task

🍎 Procedure (if it needs to be done a particular way)

🍎 Time frame for completion

🍎 Structural details

🍎 The review and completion

Day by day more detailed information can be explained as needed. Post a copy in the classroom for students to refer to when you are not available. That places responsibility for the entire project on the students.

In the following example, a third grade group is creating a detailed USA map with geographical features. You'll have one 45 to 60 minute session each week over the next four weeks. Plan out how you will divide up the task and monitor student progress. Notice the inclusion of extremely specific details in each day's directions.

The overview (first day)

"Our task is to create a colorful map of the USA. It will show the mountain ranges, major rivers, the plains, the deserts and large forested areas. Look over the printed details I have given to each of you. This is called a rubric; it lists the details that must be included when you turn in your map in four weeks."

The procedure for the task

"This project has specific directions on how your map will look. Today, we will research the atlases and discuss how to make the map easy to read. We will try to match currently-used cartographer colors."

Five Points of a Rubric

- Overview of the task

- Procedure (if it needs to be done a particular way)

- Time frame for completion

- Structural details

- The review and completion

91

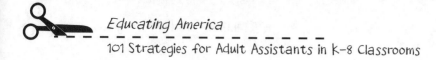

The time frame

"As we begin our research, we'll decide which features to include: mountains, rivers, plains, deserts and forests. You may add features, but make certain you include all the features mentioned on the rubric. During our next two group sessions, we'll use colored pencils to distinguish those features. By the end of the fourth week, you will need a completed map. If you require more time, use study hour. I'll turn the maps into the teacher on (date due)."

The structural details (second and third days)

"We will only use #2 and colored pencils as we recreate cartographer colors similar to the ones we've seen in various atlases.

"When you are coloring the map, use the side of the colored pencils to get an even color. If you decide to press hard, you will find it takes a lot more time, energy and pencils. That's your choice. You will need to use the #2 pencil to name all the mountains, rivers, plains, deserts and forests. Only capitalize the first letter of each proper noun, such as the 'M' and the first 'R' in Mississippi River. Be certain we can read those place names.

"Once you start writing in one direction, keep all words going that same direction. Make an accurate map key that shows the meaning of your colors."

The review and completion (fourth day)

"Let's check your rubric and review your work so far. We've colored a map with geographic features of the USA using colored pencils. We have labeled the features and started each title word with a capital letter. We've printed all titles in the same direction. Today, check over your map, then exchange with another student to evaluate each other's work. At the end of today's group, I'll be turning in your maps to the teacher for assessment."

The more details you provide for the students, the greater their chances of producing a project that meets the goals and expectations. When there are no secrets, the level of success as well as personal best increases dramatically.

How will I introduce new materials?

New materials often hold a fascination for students, especially when they are materials that can be manipulated such as maps, globes, building cubes, locking blocks, weights and measures, money and attribute blocks. If you don't give them time to explore the materials before they need to use them, they'll do it while you want them to listen to directions or perform a task.

Allow time for exploration. This means time to "muddle" with the materials, exploring their size, shape, color and use. Let them talk about their discoveries.

Think of yourself in a class, opening a new book about your favorite hobby. If you were expected to start at page one and not look ahead, you'd be disappointed and frustrated. You'd probably look ahead "on the sly," sneaking a peak when others were talking. Students feel the same way.

Allow students time to explore new materials before you begin working with them.

Allow at least ten minutes to investigate new materials before you explain their intended use; longer for young students. Most students will then set aside the materials when asked. However, if the group or individuals continue exploring and you're ready to begin the activity, you may need to collect everything and set it aside so the students will focus. Demonstrate their use. Talk

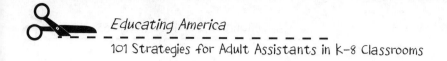

about how the materials will solve problems, will be used to make comparisons, weigh or measure objects, etc. The Exploration Guidelines chart, found at the end of the chapter and downloadable from www.PaddyEger.com will help you navigate new materials with your students.

Encourage the students to ask questions. Next, explain the guidelines for exploring and using the new materials:

1. Share the materials with others.

2. If there are many pieces, take only a few at a time.

3. Work appropriately with the materials.

4. Share your discoveries when asked.

5. Dismantle your own materials; let others dismantle theirs.

6. Put your materials away in a quiet and orderly manner.

How much of the task needs to be completed each day?

Different tasks need different levels of completion. In small groups, you can monitor progress closely and help students reach those goals.

A practice paper is not usually assessed or turned in. Practice indicates a new concept or skill. Students have had no formal exposure to the ideas or skills before this activity. They will be "trying it on for size." There should be no expectation of mastery and no expectation of students completing the task. Practice work is often ungraded, self-corrected and sent home to share with parents to inform them of the newest skill being introduced.

Reinforcing work is done after a skill or concept has been introduced and practiced. An assistant will often mark corrections and use the information to determine what skills need to be developed next. Students are encourage to complete the task. Their work may become a baseline to determine how well a concept is understood. Reinforcing pages are usually turned into the assistant or teacher.

Assessment work occurs after completion of multiple practice and reinforcing tasks. It requires students to complete the work to the best of their ability. The teacher uses the information to evaluate student learning. It may be kept for use when reporting student progress to parents.

Enrichment work demonstrates how well a student applies what is learned. It is done independently and shows how a student merges information or creates new connections. Evaluations and the need to complete the task will vary.

Does the allotted time match the group needs?

Plan your work schedule with each group to determine how much you will be able to complete in each session. Don't expect your timing to be accurate; you are working with real people who experience built-in daily differences. However, if you have taken the time to think through the needs and skills of each group, you won't be surprised when the first group only completes ⅔, the second completes ⅓ and the last group finishes with time to spare.

Let's investigate the needs of the three diverse groups we'll call 'A', 'B' and 'C.' Consider each group's strength and needs as you plan. For this activity let's assume they started work during an earlier group time.

Group 'A' consistently completes ⅔ of any task. They ask lots of questions and need detailed directions repeated more than once before they begin. How you will plan their task?

First, briefly remind them of the activity. Move around, helping individual students as needed so you can dedicate as much time as possible to working. Consider this time line:

Group 'A' completes ⅔ in a 30-minute group

1 minute for a "hook" to focus the group

5 minutes to re-introduce the lesson using brief directions

20 minutes to work with 1-2 reminders during the activity

3 minutes for clean-up

1 minute to close the lesson

Group 'B' seldom finishes more than half of any task. They work slowly but with understanding. If they are pressured, they become frustrated. Ask the teacher to select the most important parts of the task. For example, the review page has 8-10 problems, but if the students do #1, 2, 4 and 6, that exposes the basic concept. It is better if the students do a reduced portion well than to have them rush through the entire activity without understanding.

Group 'B' learns best through reviewing a task. Play with simple ideas that engage the students and build their confidence. For a specific example, let's look at Group 'B' working on alphabetizing words from a story. Any or all of these ideas will reinforce that skill.

(1) Look for objects around the classroom that begin with 'a', 'b', etc.

(2) Place the story words on cards and ask students to arrange them in a-b-c order.

(3) Play the add-on memory game: "I'm going on a trip and I'm taking…an apple, and a banana etc.". Add a new word for the next alphabet letter.

FYI: Alphabetizing student names may be tempting but is ill-advised. Multiple student names beginning with 'B-r', 'T-o' or 'D-a' will confuse struggling students. Save name alphabetizing for later, when you are working with second, third or even fourth letter alphabetizing.

Group 'B' completes ⅓ in a 30-minute group
    2 minutes for a "hook" to focus the group

    5 minutes to introduce the lesson with a revised goal

    2 minutes to answer their questions

    15 minutes to work with 1-2 reminders during activity

    3 minutes for clean-up

    3 minutes to close the lesson and share their ideas

Our hypothetical Group 'C' is focused on most every task. They grasp a concept quickly and complete activities in near record time. During group time, provide related materials or discussions to enrich their understanding. Do not hand them busy work. When you enrich the task for Group 'C', it reduces your work; you'll add depth, not create extra tasks to evaluate, so it will keep the three diverse groups focused on the same tasks during the same weeks.

Group 'C' finishes quickly and accurately in a 30-minute group
    2 minutes for a "hook" to focus the group/expand ideas

    6 minutes to review the lesson/elaborate/discuss/share work

    2 minutes for new activity directions

    14 minutes to work with 1-2 reminders during activity

    3 minutes for clean-up

    3 minutes to close the lesson

All groups develop a working rhythm. Find that rhythm and organize your activity and time to match it. The students will use their time more wisely, accomplish more, and come away feeling greater success.

Within a group, you may want or need to modify a task for individual students. Let's look at Mary, James and Tom:

Mary knows how to do the task, but her meticulous printing slows her down. Help her by becoming her scribe. She can tell you what to write for a few minutes to give her a break. Then turn it back to her to complete.

Every group has a working rhythm. Organize your activity and time to match.

James rushes through to be first. Remind him that you want quality work and that he needs to slow down to produce his personal best. Check back with him several times to be certain he hasn't raced through his work the minute you turn your attention to another student.

Tom struggles to finish when he works at his normal speed. Look over the task. Have Tom complete the most important parts first. Then, as he has time, he can go back and fill in the rest. This won't work for a sequential task. In that instance, team him up with a stronger student. Send them to a nearby area to work, where they can talk together and not disturb others. Shared thinking for five to ten minutes will help Tom get started.

Don't penalize the stronger student by keeping them together for the entire task. Let each return to working independently after a few minutes of shared time. You can check Tom's progress. Be ready to assist him, but don't take over his task.

Personal best may differ for each task and each individual. Sometimes you need to help students work to meet your expectations. Adjust the assignment so students don't feel rushed or become frustrated, but never do the work for a student. Doing this negates the student's confidence and sends a message that he or she isn't capable of working independently. It may also encourage a student to disengage thinking, because you often step in and finish the work.

If your entire group is struggling, either shorten the task or let them complete the task the next time you meet. When students are hurried, the quality of their work drops and the value of the task may disappear as well.

How can students self-monitor their work?

As work time begins, discuss the following questions.

Before I begin my work...
   What is my task today?
   What questions do I have before I start working?
   What help do I need from the adult leader?

After I finish my work for today:
   What have I done well on this task?
   What changes might I consider making?
   Is this quality work?

Copy these questions and display them for student use. A reproducible copy may be found at the end of this chapter or downloaded from www.PaddyEger.com.

How will I handle off-task behavior?

Keeping students focused depends on remembering to:

- Review your expectations weekly with your groups.
- Reinforce behavior through compliments to on-task students.

🍎 Refocus off-task students; check their work for complete answers or ask them to share their best work aloud.

🍎 Talk with the teacher if your attempts to refocus students don't work.

Keep a simple activity handy, to use when you finish tasks early.

How do I accommodate students who finish early?

Plan ahead if it is important to keep your group with you and working until a designated time. Remember, if you let your group leave early, other groups may think it is time to go and become antsy or leave their groups before the designated time. That can get chaotic.

Keep a simple pocket activity handy; something that requires minimal materials and directions. For younger student groups who finish early:

🍎 Draw a personal experience related to the activity

🍎 Read a related book or article

🍎 Work on a group puzzle

With older students:

🍎 Brainy card packs

🍎 Lateral thinking questions

🍎 Word searches and crosswords related to the activity

Even though you may never need to use pocket activities, being prepared is easier than scampering for one at the last minute.

How do I assist slower students and keep them independent?

Time management is a factor for slower workers. To help them stay on task, write a schedule of your expectations on paper or on the board. Assign times beside the activities to help them stay on task and develop their time management.

Example of a schedule on the board:

2:00-2:20 Problems 1-4 completed
(allow 3-5 minutes a problem)

2:25 Math Journal collected; begin Independent Math

2:50 Independent Math packet turned in

When students work hard and need every moment to finish a task, we often forget to give them time for independent activities. Check over the current task to see if the slower workers can skip part of a problem without compromising their learning. Remember to acknowledge their effort by providing time to work on the independent activities. Everyone deserves a change of pace after working diligently.

Exploration Guidelines for New Materials

Demonstrate use of the new materials:

- Talk about how these materials will solve problems, be used to make comparisons, weigh or measure objects.

- Let the students ask questions.

- Set your expectations.

- Explain the guidelines for using the new materials, such as:

- Share the materials with others.

- If there are many pieces, take only a few at a time.

- Work appropriately with the materials.

- Share your discoveries when asked.

- Dismantle your own materials.

- Let others dismantle theirs.

- Put materials away in a quiet and orderly manner.

Figure 7.1—Exploration Guidelines for New Materials

Student Self-Monitor Checklist

Before I begin my work...

What is my task today?

What questions do I have before I start working?

What help do I need from the adult leader?

After I finish my work for today...

What have I done well on this task?

What changes might I consider making?

Is this quality work?

Figure 7.2—Student Self-Monitor Checklist

Clarify Details

Students need you to set clear guidelines and procedures so they can complete their tasks. Consider the following questions:

How will I begin my activity?
Do students understand my expectations for the lesson?
Do I have a positive attitude about the activity?
Do I allow time for students to think before they answer?
Do I value one specific answer or a variety of responses?
How will I assess student understanding of the task?
Is it acceptable to work with peers?
How will I ensure a quiet work time?
What is quality work for this activity?
What is the quality of thought?
Do I use the 5-minute reminder?
What is quality of printing or writing?

How will I begin my activity?

When students first arrive, introduce the task with a "hook": a related item such as a news article, a riddle, an artifact, a game or part of a book/poem. The intent is to focus student attention and give stragglers a chance to settle in before the planned activity begins. Keep the hook brief and related to the current activity. You will find further information on Hooks to Snag Student Interest in the Appendix as well as on www.PaddyEger.com.

In our primary classroom a hand puppet helped a frustrated assistant. Week after week, she'd had problems getting students to sit down and focus. Once the puppet became her hook, the students came quickly and quietly to "talk" with the puppet and learn the day's task. They settled into their activity quickly and completed more during their group time.

Taking time to create an interesting introduction for a task adds energy and interest. Do not spend so much time on focusing the students that you forget to start the task for the day. And, if your group is already focused, set aside the hook or keep it short.

Do students understand my expectations for the lesson?

Don't leave students guessing. After you introduce an activity, share your specific task and behavioral expectations.

Examples:

"Today we are writing a short story about what you enjoyed during winter break. This is a time to work and think alone, so I expect everyone to use a level zero voice. If you need help, raise your thumb."

"This is a first draft. We will do an edit today then write a final, quality copy to hand in to the teacher next week. It will become part of your writing portfolio."

"Our goal today is to create a list of how we use magnets. We'll take turns sharing ideas by passing the roll of tape. When you hold the roll, tell us your best magnet idea. The rest of the time, actively listen with your eyes on the speaker and your bodies still. I'll be your scribe. Our list will be displayed along with other groups' ideas for the class to read and discuss next week."

"There are lots of ways to make '12.' Think of a great equation. Whisper share it with the persons on your right and left." (Here the group would share and discuss their ideas.) "Your personal task is to write down as many ways to make '12' as you can think of in the next ten minutes. Be creative; don't worry about the quality of your printing today. Check your ideas to be certain each equals '12.' You'll use your ideas for a project."

Notice the inclusion of the information the students needed to understand the level of work expected for the activity. Each of these issues were addressed:

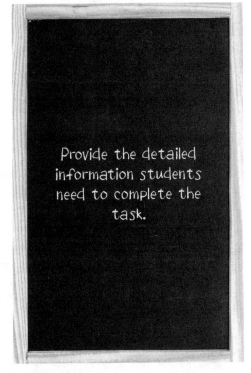

Provide the detailed information students need to complete the task.

(1) Time allowed for the activity:

    🖉 Do I need to complete this today?

    🖉 May I continue on during my study time?

    🖉 May I finish this the next time we meet?

(2) The quality of work expected:

    🖉 Is this a practice task to gather my ideas?

    🖉 Is this a work-in-progress that will be revised later?

    🖉 Is there a rubric or a set of guidelines I need to follow?

    🖉 Is my best quality printing/writing expected?

(3) How the work will be assessed:

    🖉 Will I check my own work?

    🖉 Will an adult check my work and send it home today?

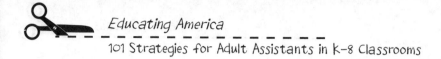
🖋 Will an adult check my work and return it next time?

🖋 Will the task be given to the teacher to assess?

🖋 Is this work part of my progress report?

The more information you provide, the better chance they have to meet your expectations.

Remember to make it safe for students to ask for clarification during the activity. Stop after five minutes to check their understanding. Answer their questions and have students share. You might be surprised to find that what you think you said and what they heard are not the same thing.

Do I have a positive attitude about the activity?

Saying, "I know this is boring but the teacher says you have to do it" isn't a good idea. Or saying, "I know this is too hard for you, so just do any you know" negates their skills. So, how do you handle your attitude?

If you truly feel the activity is too easy, too hard or extraneous, talk with the teacher. Many times classroom activities spiral; a skill is introduced, practiced and then repeated with a twist.

As adults, we often see this as boring or repetitive. That may be true for us, but that very repetition helps develop student skills. When we say it is boring or too hard, we undermine the classroom teacher and devalue the teacher's plan for the class.

Naming your groups "the high group" or "the crows" (or something that implies comparison and demeans the groups) demonstrates a lack of sensitivity. Students understand they are working at different levels, and most try their best. We want them to feel positive about their effort. Comments that create negative feelings for students have no place in the classroom.

Adult body language and facial gestures are another way a child evaluates the task. If you look or act cross or bored, children often mimic your attitude and the quality of their work diminishes. You are their leader; present the task with enthusiasm. Explain why they are doing the activity and what they will learn by doing it. Your attitude may determine the quality of each student's work.

Example:

"Today we are practicing math facts. These games are lots of fun and they will help you think fast. Remember, everyone wins when they know their facts and don't have to stop and count every time."

Do I allow time for students to think before they answer?

Most of us appreciate time to think before we answer. Children need that same consideration. In education it is called "wait time." This quiet moment gives students time to process rather than shoot their hand into the air and be "first." Wait time lasts five, ten, or fifteen seconds. Most students are able to process a question and select a reasonable answer in that amount of time.

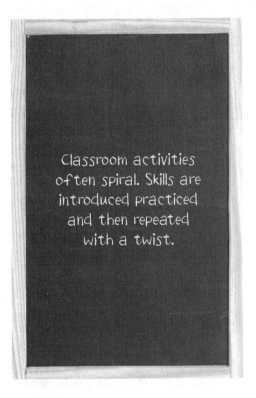

Classroom activities often spiral. Skills are introduced practiced and then repeated with a twist.

Example:

"Close your eyes and think inside your head. What four ways can you build the number '10'? When you are ready, open your eyes and raise your thumb on the table. Don't say anything until I call for answers. If someone shares your idea, have a second idea ready. Be creative. Ready? Set? Think."

Wait time encourages more students to take an academic risk. If you incorporate a "thumb up" or "think a minute" approach in your group, the quiet allows more students to formulate appropriate answers. For a shy or unsure student it allows much needed time to generate an answer.

When you first use wait time, it feels like you are waiting for hours. But, if you incorporate it into your activity on a regular basis, more and more students will be able to participate. Best answers rather than first answers are stronger answers.

Intermix your question and answer techniques. Begin with reluctant learners to allow them a chance to answer early on. This also benefits quick thinkers. If they wait longer to answer, quick thinkers often create more intricate or complex answers which keep them engaged.

Using note cards with student names for each group, passing the roll of tape, and other previously mentioned approaches keeps the group focused. Remember, school is not a race that encourages students to be first. It's a place where we want all students to have time to think so they will participate in a meaningful way.

Do I value one specific answer or a variety of responses?

Use of open-ended or multiple answer questions promotes creative thinking. If the traditional question is "Name the capital of Washington," change and ask, "How do you think the capital of Washington got its name?" If the traditional question is "What does a thermometer do?" Rephrase it to, "When do people use thermometers?" If the traditional question is "Who is the main character in the story?" Rephrase it to, "What does the main character do that makes him so important in the story?"

Changing to open-ended questions invites all students in your group to participate at their own level. And, having a wide variety of possible answers energizes a group.

Give it a try. Change these single answer questions to questions with multiple answers. When is Independence Day? Who was the first President of the United States? How much is 10+7? Where is China on the map? Name the first month of the year. What season comes after winter? The possibilities are endless.

How will I assess student understanding of the task?

Be watchful. Check in with each student periodically. Share student work and ideas briefly when you do your 5-minute check-up, then send the group back to work. If possible, save time at the end of the activity to share student ideas. Remember, shy students don't ask for help even when they feel lost.

Encourage students to share specific ideas rather than everything they have done. Ask for opening sentences, best sentences, best ideas or new information they learned as they worked. Discuss things they might change to improve their work. If you had difficulty explaining an activity, ask for student input about how you could present the directions in a more understandable way next time.

Use of open-ended or multiple answer questions promotes creative thinking.

Is it acceptable to work with peers?

Peer assistance is often better than adult assistance because students speak the same language. They "see" things in similar ways, and helping others often reinforces their own understanding of a task. Because we have vast life and school experiences, we forget that most students require detailed information before they begin

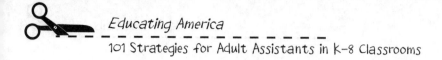
a task. It is vital to go through the basic directions then use student input to clarify the task before the group begins work.

If a student acts lost or confused, ask another student to re-state the directions. Mary can help James get started by telling him what she is doing first and what she will do next.

Example:

"Okay, James. I am going to put my name on the top line. Then I am going to write a sentence about what I want to do for my science project. Last, I'll tell the teacher what supplies I need."

Once Mary helps James get started, you step in to support him. That way Mary can get back to work. When you use students as helpers this way, it is important they receive enough time to do their own work. Do not abuse this strategy. Students will refuse to help others if you always expect them to act as tutors when they need to focus on their own task.

If you need assistance giving directions, listen to the way students break down the activity for others. Use their style of explana-tions. Still need help? Talk with the teacher.

How will I ensure a quiet work time?

Use the classroom expectations. Give clear directions, answer questions, remind students to monitor their voices, then send them to work.

Example:

"While you work on this project, I expect you will respect others by working quietly using a Level 1 or 2 voice and by sharing ma-terials. If you have a question, raise your thumb and I will come over to talk with you.

"As you finish, scan your work and make changes. I'll check your work and return it to you next time we meet. If you finish early, your choices are to use your free reading book or work on your folder cover design."

What is quality work for this activity?

Teachers stress quality work which is neat and complete, shows clear thinking, and represents the student's personal best. This does not mean perfect work. It means well thought out work.

Personal best is the goal in most classrooms. This varies from one student to another and is based on their skills as much as how well they understand the activity. It includes but is not limited to:

- Work that demonstrates understanding of the task
- Clear or logical thinking
- Complete sentences
- Legible printing or writing
- Appropriate punctuation
- Appropriate capitalization
- Proper use of headings
- Proofed or edited work
- Completed tasks

Personal best can be further broken down into two components: quality of thought and quality of printing or writing. Both are valuable, but quality of thought is our daily focus in the classroom.

What is quality of thought?

Quality of thought is a student's ability to expresses on-topic ideas that are organized and pertinent. All types of activities from discussions to practice pages to final draft research incorporate active thinking which leads to quality of thought.

While personal stories can be part of the thinking process, students need to learn when and where personal experiences are important to share. Step in when "stories" replace pertinent thoughts and redirect the discussions.

Example:

"Mary, I'm glad you had fun at the park, but we want you to tell us which activity in the science park you enjoyed the most. You'll have time to write about your trip later."

Using 5-minute reminders and sharing student work helps students understand this goal. All students benefit from hearing others' ideas as well as sharing their work-in-progress. For some, sharing represents a huge risk, but it is important to keep students talking, sharing and thinking.

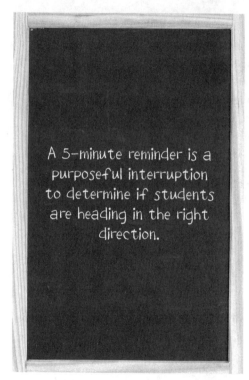

A 5-minute reminder is a purposeful interruption to determine if students are heading in the right direction.

Do I use the 5-minute reminder?

The 5-minute reminder is a purposeful, brief interruption. It is a check-in time to determine if students are headed in the correct direction on the task.

Five minutes into a task, instruct students to set down their pencils and other tools. Ask a brief question to check their understanding of the task.

Examples:

"Who can tell me what we are expected to do today?"

"Who will share how you started today's activity?"

"What questions have come up as you've started to work?"

This reminder helps redirect a student who has misunderstood the task. It saves the student from a total redo since the error is caught early into the activity.

During the 5-minute reminder, you can point out special or strong elements that shared work demonstrates, or restate details. Often, students are inspired to revise their ideas.

When the entire group wants to share ideas, select one or two students. At the end of the activity, take time to hear from the rest of the group. While sharing at the end takes away from the group work time, but it's an important part of learning and worth every minute.

What is quality of printing or writing?

Quality of printing or writing focuses on the visual presentation of the task. Its importance varies from practice sheets to research papers. When students are learning a new skill or practicing, the quality of printing is never as important as the quality of thought.

On longer tasks, once student thoughts are organized and the first draft is written, students need to focus on the appearance of the finished paper. This is often the least favorite step because it signals a "rewrite." So, if a rewrite is necessary, mention that fact during the directions. Be prepared for moans and groans.

Don't try to do a rewrite in one sitting, because the quality of writing, especially for young students, will suffer. Break down the rewrite task into sections. Have students read their opening paragraphs. Discuss their varied approaches, then have them rewrite that first paragraph. Move on to the next paragraph and repeat the procedure.

Example:

"Our animal reports have several parts. First read and take notes. Then write the information in your own words. Next, you and I will read over each section of the report and see what changes are needed.

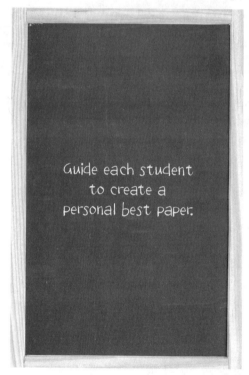

Guide each student to create a personal best paper.

"We will do a complete rewrite to fix spelling errors, rearrange your thoughts and add details to enhance the report. After each part is edited, you will rewrite it using your best writing skills. Then you will have time to illustrate that section before you move on to the following section. This report will be shared with your parents at open house."

On lengthy projects make it clear to all students that you will only accept their best work on the final draft. Do not rush or penalize slow workers who need extra time to produce a finished project. Plan an enhancing, independent activity for those who finish early. Be certain slow workers have a chance to work on the additional activity when time allows.

To demonstrate quality of printing or writing, direct each student to create a personal best paper, an example of their best printing/writing. Save this "best" paper and use it as a mirror for future tasks. When a project is completed, place it beside the personal best paper and compare the two for neatness and writing conventions (punctuation, capitalization, sentence structure). Ask the students to decide if the project represents their personal best. If they say "yes," point out the strengths. If the project work is sloppy or lacks organization, point out the specific changes needed to create an acceptable paper.

As an individual's personal best grows and changes the "best" paper is replaced by new samples that demonstrate improved work quality. What a powerful tool: a new personal best paper replacing an earlier one! Over time these samples lead to an improved quality of work that each student can self-judge.

Quality takes time. When you work with a group for a while, setting standards becomes easier. You'll be able to pace activities to match individual or specific group needs. Coupled with a quiet work environment and clear work expectations, the results are worth the effort.

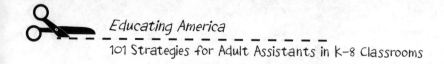

Wrap-Up

Ending an activity requires as much planning and organization as beginning an activity. You need to keep students focused until they leave the group. Consider these questions:

Who is responsible for clean-up?
How do I get closure on my activity?
How do I excuse the students from my group?
How do I evaluate my group's progress?
Have I followed classroom procedures?

Who is responsible for clean-up?

When your group uses the materials, your group needs to clean them up. Take time to develop student responsibility for their supplies and materials. All ages can help; most student groups can do the entire clean-up if you include adequate time in your overall plan. Include:

- Handing work to (rather than tossing it toward)you
- Collecting work papers, equipment, and supplies quietly
- Picking up debris and supplies from the floor
- Restacking books
- Wiping down tables for the next group

In most schools, custodians do not clean every room every evening. Even if they do, morning groups need to keep things picked up so afternoon groups can begin with a clean workspace. Afternoon groups need to leave clean workspaces for the next morning's groups.

When you have an especially messy project, allow extra clean-up time. Think ahead; what is needed for an effective clean-up? Have your tools ready: sponges, paper towels, supply containers.

Pick up cut paper scraps from the table in a small tub every few minutes during the work period. It keeps the workspace tidy and will save time during clean up at the end.

Books should be stacked, not tossed toward the pile. Stack all books with like books and pile them facing the same direction for the next group.

Papers and workbooks, like books, need to be turned in, not tossed to you. If student names are on the front and the papers are closed to the front page, they will be ready for next time. It takes two seconds for a child to close booklets and hand them to you in an orderly manner. You can rubber band them and set them aside. Also, if you have work projects continuing on, use a different colored folder for each group's materials to stay organized.

Glue can be controlled by not giving students entire containers. Instead give them very small quantities such as a puddle on a wax paper square. Two students share the puddle. When the group ends, the small papers are folded inward to wrap in the glue before tossing them into the garbage. New wax papers can be given to each pair of students.

Some adults create a system so individual students perform specific jobs. Their work is done in a short time with minimal adult supervision. Remember to give a hearty "Thank You."

In one kindergarten classroom I observed, the student project included yarn, scissors, pencils, buttons, paper plates, crayons, cut paper in various sizes and colors, glitter and glue. If the assistants had elected to clean up all the supplies and put them away, it would have taken more than fifteen minutes. With the help of the children and supply tubs with labels and specific shelves for everything, the students quietly put away all of the items and wiped down the tables in under four minutes! They beamed when the adults thanked them. Plan ahead!

Remember, clean-up is an important part of every task, even at school.

When an activity ends, proceed in a calm, controlled manner. If you end abruptly or let students get up and walk off without helping, you'll be facing chaos and a huge mess, alone.

Example:

"Books go on my right, right side up and not tossed. Pencils go in the tub. Papers are closed with your name showing. Don't toss them, lay them in my basket. Hand the folders to…Check the floor for dropped materials. When you have finished, sit down and look at me."

Now you are in control. Everything is organized so you have time for closure on your activity.

Clean-up is a student responsibility—

Plan ahead!

How do I get closure on my activity?

If you let the students walk away after clean-up, you'll have skipped closure, an important part of the activity. It's like the end credits of a movie. It gives you a moment to reflect on the entire experience before you move on. This is a short yet vital activity: a time to ask questions, review the task and compliment successes.

Examples:

"What did you enjoy about today's task?"

"What worked well for you today?"

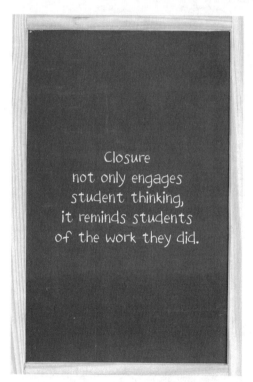

Closure
not only engages
student thinking,
it reminds students
of the work they did.

"What questions do you have about what we did today?"

"Which students in our group would you like to compliment?"

A brief discussion engages student thinking. It reminds students of the work they did with you and that you place value on the activity.

How do I excuse the students from my group?

Create an ending routine that keeps the students calm and well-mannered as they move to another activity. Unstructured transitions from one group to another may lead to students acting crazy, slugging, pushing, or shoving each other. Teachers expect students to behave during transitions.

Example:

"Thank you for participating, and cleaning up. After you push in your chairs, I want you to move quietly to your next activity without bumping into other students. (For young students add: "I'll watch you move to their next activity." When they look back give them a thumb up and a smile to reinforce their appropriate behavior.)

Now, take a calming breath and get ready for the next group. If you've made your expectations clear, the next group will stand and wait by your table until you invite them to sit down. The work area was cleaned up by the exiting group, so the new group has a tidy place to work. All materials are organized, the same as for the first group.

How do I evaluate my group's progress?

Many teachers want information on how the individual groups functioned. They want to know who cooperated, who learned new things, who was helpful and who frustrated the group. Take the time to jot the teacher a note or fill out a group evaluation form if one is provided. Writing "It was a great group." doesn't tell the teacher enough. Take two minutes and be specific. Begin with student achievements and successes. Mention "what worked" and any problems or concerns.

Student work needs to be evaluated. Check practice pages and first attempts to understand what problems the students experienced and what modifications the group needs.

No one enjoys seeing their work marked up. Use a sticky note for comments to students. Circle the numbers of problems that need rechecking, so that the student can rework the problem and your circle can become 'o-k' when you add the 'k' after the initial circle marking unless told otherwise let the teacher assign grades.

Math Group 3

The math facts group finished several tasks and worked well together. Many calculated the answers in their heads. James and Tom had to use paper and pencil and needed extra time to complete the problems. They may need to change groups or spend time reviewing their basic facts. We need part of another day to complete today's activity. Is there a game early finishers might play to reinforce their facts?

Have I followed classroom procedures?

Your activities for the day have ended. It's time to give yourself a mental check-up. You should have:

- Introduced the lesson
- Explained your expectations
- Lead the group
- Assisted students
- Supervised clean up
- Taken time for a brief closing discussion
- Dismissed students in an orderly manner
- Evaluated student work and group progress
- Looked over your next activity for copies/supplies
- Put away materials
- Turned in group evaluations

Some classrooms have assistant desks to use for planning, evaluating or helping with classroom projects. If you see an activity that needs finishing or papers to collate, and you have time, stay and work on them. If there is a take home project, leave the teacher a note and take the project home. Deliver it back to school one full day before the teacher's requested date. Should you not be able to finish the project in a timely manner, find someone to assist you, but get the project back on time. Unfinished or missing projects will foul up the teacher's plans and activities.

Teachers value your assistance on projects. Your willingness to help translates to one to two hours that the teacher can spend on school, family or personal activities. Read that as a huge 'thank you'.

Leave the classroom quietly when your tasks are completed. Your help has given the teacher and students three wonderful gifts: your time, your energy and your love of learning.

Mostly for Teachers

When a teacher begins the process of including adult assistants, several items must be considered: planning, implementing or training and supporting the people who step forward to perform these functions. The initial task is overwhelming, but the benefits for the students as well as the teacher are powerful. The ratio of adults to students moves from 1:26 (one teacher for 26 students) to 1:13 with one helper, 1:5 if several small groups are working at the same time and 1:1 when students are paired with assistants. The time spent to set up and use assistants is worth every minute.

Plan for Adult Assistants

Utilizing assistants takes an extreme amount of thought and organization. Consider what tasks you are willing to relinquish to an assistant. The worksheet 101 Jobs Adults Can Do to Assist Teachers provides a starting point. This and other forms mentioned in this chapter are located in the Appendix and are downloadable from www.PaddyEger.com

Start small. Arrange for assistants to ease into your classroom over the first month. This will give you time to plan their lessons, observe their groups, and monitor and adjust their tasks. See the Planning for Adult Assistants worksheet for ideas.

Decide whether you want to use the assistants as flexible rovers, tutors, or small group leaders. This decision is a matter of personal style and your level of comfort with assistants in the classroom.

In our school, adult assistants help several hours a day, every day. They perform a variety of tasks from taking attendance to gathering materials for projects to leading small groups.

Our assistants directed small groups working on map skills, reading enrichment, creative writing, spelling, dictionary skills, math facts, social studies topics, computer training, science projects, research, experimental art/crafts and much, much more. In many instances, their assignments matched their interests and skills. See the Adult Assistant Inventory provided in the index.

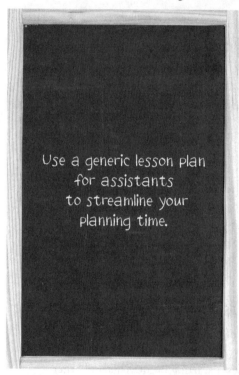

Use a generic lesson plan for assistants to streamline your planning time.

Determine which days of the week you want assistants, when each should arrive and how long each is expected to work. Creating a consistent time and task helps assistants plan for baby-sitters, paid work outside the classroom and other personal scheduling issues.

Use a generic lesson plan to streamline the amount of time needed for planning. Two are provided in the index. One is a basic plan, the other includes extensive details.

Plan out activities for at least one week in advance of when your assistants will need them. Keep copies of their tasks, projects and materials organized in folders or notebooks. Once a week check the folders. It is imperative that you monitor student work and progress, adjust materials, assess goals for the assistants, and understand when it is time to change groups and plan new activities. Write notes to the adult assistants mentioning your concerns, ideas for changes as well as up-coming activities.

I found it easier to plan entire units of study for assistants. This meant spending several days going through objectives, setting my goals, organizing materials and activities, and writing up a plan. By doing this I was able to see the entire scope and sequence for each group through the year, and the assistants were able to see this as well.

Create evaluation forms for your assistants to use when they end group activities. These provide important feedback. A sample form is provided at the end of the chapter entitled Deal with Misbehavior.

Train Adult Assistants

Organize an information meeting or workshop. Plan to spend a huge amount of time planning; try to squeeze as much as possible into one meeting. The more prepared you are, the better the chance your assistants will understand your goals. If you want everyone's attendance, give them a "heads up" regarding the date and time as early as possible. Share the information in one two-hour sitting, including questions and answers. That allows you to explain the details to everyone and minimizes misunderstandings.

Discuss and hand out pertinent information related to:

Classroom educational goals and expectations
Classroom subject matter for the year
Classroom rules and behavior goals
Classroom organization and procedures
Communication preferences
Adult assistant responsibilities and procedures
Assistant work schedules
Assistant work area

Classroom educational goals and expectations

Use your classroom and the school's objectives to form learning groups of no more than six students. Decide which activities adult helpers can lead without intensive direction. Avoid educational jargon when writing out your plans.

Classroom subject matter for the year

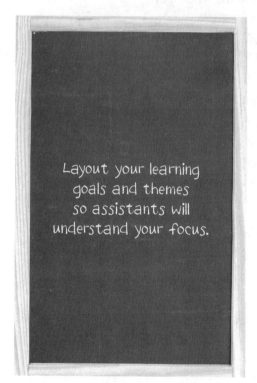

Layout your learning goals and themes so assistants will understand your focus.

Lay out your learning goals and themes for the year so assistants will understand your focus. Show how the subject matter intersects. Highlight large projects, special events, and field trips. Encourage assistants to keep a lookout for related information, activities, and ideas to incorporate into the program during the year.

Classroom rules and behavior goals

Display and discuss your classroom rules and behavior plan for all to see. Be specific. What do you expect students to do when they have questions? How and when are students excused to the rest room? How should students signal when they wish to share an idea?

Stress the need for consistency. Let them know you expect each person to model classroom rules, behavior, and voice levels for the students.

Talk about how you want misbehavior handled. Share how and when you want students brought to you to discuss their behavior. Be as specific as possible. Explain that you are the final word on misbehavior.

Classroom organization and procedures

Each teacher organizes in different ways. Share your storage preferences, the flow of the room, the grouping of desks, etc. so assistants will understand your organization.

Invite assistants to observe your classroom to watch how it functions. This observation process will teach them how you:

- Get and hold student attention
- Call on students throughout the classroom
- Lead discussions and ask questions
- Remind off-task students of classroom expectations
- Check student understanding of tasks
- Dismiss students to various activities
- Hand out materials and hand in work
- Start students working

Communication preferences

Indicate the way you prefer assistants contact you, whether by letter, e-mail, phone message, or in person. Pass out your contact information and the specific times you are available for calls. Show them where to place written notes. Let them know you will reply as soon as possible.

Create a biweekly or weekly newsletter to share up-coming events, the classroom and school calendar changes, class projects, field trips, and tips for working in the classroom. Post a newsletter online and on an assistant's information board, so it can be read at their convenience.

Adult assistant responsibilities and procedures

Let the assistants know how they will be used in the classroom. Explain when each should arrive and their individual jobs, such as rovers, small group leaders, tutors, or a combination of all three.

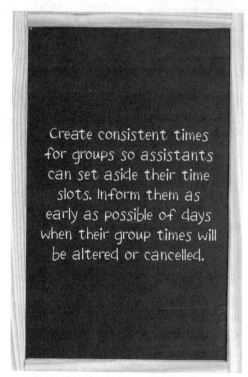

Create consistent times for groups so assistants can set aside their time slots. Inform them as early as possible of days when their group times will be altered or cancelled.

Rovers will be expected to do whatever needs doing. They need to arrive in time to watch the activity long enough to understand the goals. Rovers do jobs like reading with students, editing student writing, supervising student progress on a task, or helping with student review materials. They might also assemble science materials, collect library books for a project, or type student writing. Leave them specific written objectives for each work period.

Example:

"As students begin their research, be sure they write down the book titles they use. Also, if a student needs help reading, take that student to a work table and partner read the selection."

Small groups function to enhance your classroom objectives. When you organize them, write simple explanations of the activity and the objectives.

Example:

"The group goal: have each individual read the two stories, write new endings and share those with the rest of the group. Save their work for me to see."

List up-coming activities so assistants will know where their tasks are headed. Plan for a few weeks, a month, or for the year rather than day by day. Assistants will begin thinking of additional materials or information they can bring in to support the tasks. Pre-planning also means the assistants can move to the next activity without checking in with you every time they arrive to work in the classroom.

Gather the needed materials in tubs or folders so assistants can pick up all supplies in one trip. Let them know where replacements are stored. Show them the table or area where they are to meet their students. If possible, reserve that location for that group every week. Be sure these areas do not impede the flow of your classroom.

Once you share your expectations, assistants can effectively lead small groups. They may often enhance classroom learning by sharing their expertise in topics related to the school curriculum. To gather that information send out an interest inventory at the beginning of the school year.

Tutors work one-on-one with students and need extra training to understand how to assist struggling students. Explain that they need to take the student aside to work privately. Give them suggestions for breaking down skills, pacing their tasks and building student confidence.

Assistant work schedules

Create consistent times for groups so assistants can set aside their time slots. Inform them as early as possible of days when their group times will be altered or cancelled. If you have last minute changes, do not send them home; if they feel under utilized, they may not return. Consider these alternative activities when your regular activities have changed for the day:

🍎 Listen to a child read

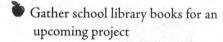

🍎 Help a child correct writing

🍎 Check student papers

🍎 File, collate student work, assemble work packets

🍎 Pass out "go home" papers

🍎 Gather school library books for an upcoming project

🍎 Organize art, science, math, and writing materials

Post work schedules on a common board so assistants can exchange work time when they have conflicts or emergencies. With their permission, share contact numbers so each can arrange their own substitutes. Impress the importance of their finding replacements so your classroom activities flow smoothly.

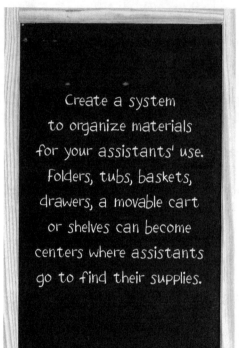

Create a system to organize materials for your assistants' use. Folders, tubs, baskets, drawers, a movable cart or shelves can become centers where assistants go to find their supplies.

Assistant work areas

Create a system to organize materials for your assistants' use. Folders, tubs, baskets, drawers, a movable cart or shelves can become a permanent "home" for classroom supplies so you, the helpers, or their substitutes can locate needed materials.

Show assistants where to hang their coats and stow their belongings. The areas around work spaces should be clear of bags, jackets and other personal belongings.

If possible, create a workspace for their use. Include a small desk with classroom supplies, like pens, paper, scissors, stapler and staples, stickers, tape, sticky notes, a student name list and your classroom schedules. Hang a small whiteboard or corkboard nearby to post the school calendar, reminders, notes to the workers and quotes.

Quick turnaround jobs can be left on or near the desk for assistants who have a few minutes. They can trim art, file student work, cut out letters for a display and so forth. Let them know at the planning workshop that their help on small projects will be deeply appreciated.

Support adult assistants

Prepare and organize materials for small groups using a generic lesson form. When a substitute comes in to work, they will know how to read the plan and will require little to no assistance from the teacher as they settle in to work.

Greet the assistants every day with a sincere welcome. Many have left sick children with neighbors or have rearranged their work day to come to the classroom. Use their time wisely and remember to thank them when they leave.

The first few weeks of using assistants, it's beneficial to walk through the class to watch and listen to how they handle activities. Make suggestions, peruse student work, observe student work habits. Note how the assistants give directions, offer positive feedback, and keep students on task. Praise their successes and restate your expectations when things move off-track or when groups are getting too loud.

After the assistants have worked in class for a few weeks, check periodically to be sure they are using your suggestions and that their interactions are appropriate. When you look through their work folders each week, you can determine the the success of the task just completed as well as individual student progress.

Write clear, concise directions and attach them to the work. Hang up a permanent list of ways they can help students and the classroom. See the ideas on the worksheet *What Can I Do?* included in the Appendix and available for download at www. PaddyEger.com.

Getting started is the hard part. At first glance, it's overwhelming. But imagine the extra activities you can include when you have trained, interested adults working with you! Once you provide direction, explain their tasks, and help them organize their activities, you will become comfortable working together.

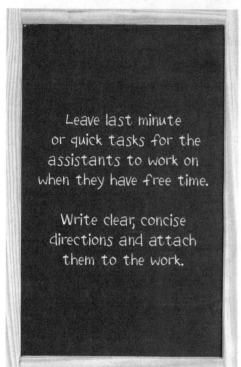

Leave last minute or quick tasks for the assistants to work on when they have free time.

Write clear, concise directions and attach them to the work.

Adult assistants also ease your work load by changing the adult to child ratio. As a teacher who has worked alone with thirty students and then had multiple assistants in my classroom, I believe the work organizing the adults and their groups is worth every minute spent. Students soar with the increased interaction and enhanced learning that trained assistants bring into the classroom.

Throughout the school year hold brief retraining sessions. Introduce questioning strategies, thinking skills, and way to enhance student learning. Invite them to share their successes and tips for working with students.

Overwhelmed? Need two aspirin after reading this? Doubt you can organize to do all this? Read through the worksheets in the Appendix before you decide and visit www.PaddyEger.com for discussions and additional information.

Mostly for Adult Assistants

Participation in classrooms has come a long way from parents and other adults bringing napkins and treats for a class party or attending school concerts. Today, active adults:

- Prepare class projects
- Assist with small groups
- Organize classroom and school committees
- Organize and attend field trips
- Share their expertise and interests with students

The following content is a brief overview to reinforce what you have just read in the earlier chapters of this book. Our focus, working in classrooms, requires assistants to partner with and work to support the teacher's curriculum and class guidelines. To become a positive-thinking educational helper:

Ask the teacher for guidance.
Observe the teacher working with students.
Model active listening.
Prepare before your work time begins.
Become familiar with school-specific details.
Use positive communication and genuine praise.

Keep your activity moving forward.
Carry a pocket activity.
Handle transitions.
Know the policy for leaving students unsupervised.
Practice safe behaviors.
Treat the teacher's desk as a private space.
Be positive, helpful, and supportive of the classroom and school.
Put away supplies and materials.
Start fresh, each day, with all students.
Maintain confidentiality.
Support teachers by helping with small tasks.
Leave cell phones and electronic devices off or on vibrate.
Know that you are appreciated by teachers, students, and other adults.

Ask the teacher for guidance.

If the teacher offers a workshop, plan to attend and listen to suggestions. The teacher is the professional guide for the class. Learn and follow the school and classroom rules. Use all suggestions for organizing, dealing with misbehavior, and asking purposeful questions. Many charts and forms are available for your support in the Appendix and for download from www.PaddyEger.com

Working with students takes planning, clear expectations and focused objectives. You must partner with teachers, not take over the activities or change the classroom goals. Remember, 'assist' is defined as "to give support or aid."

Observe the teacher working with students.

Listen to the phrases the teacher uses to elicit information, give praise, redirect students, and prepare them to begin tasks. Model yourself after the teacher and use those techniques when working with students.

Model active listening.

Model listening to students by using eye contact and providing feedback to their questions and comments. Active listening shows your respect for the learner.

Example:

"I heard you say that you added the first two numbers and then took away the last number to reach 12."

Prepare before your work time begins.

The time you spend planning relates directly to your level of success in leading a group.

Plan the way you will explain tasks to students. Be systematic.

Give them an overview, then explain the beginning steps.

Write out other steps, breaking them into simple statements.

Become familiar with school-specific details.

Active listening shows your respect for the learner.

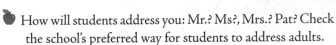 How will students address you: Mr.? Ms?, Mrs.? Pat? Check the school's preferred way for students to address adults.

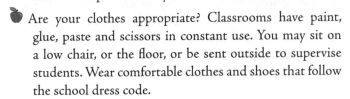 Are your clothes appropriate? Classrooms have paint, glue, paste and scissors in constant use. You may sit on a low chair, or the floor, or be sent outside to supervise students. Wear comfortable clothes and shoes that follow the school dress code.

🍎 Is the teacher's lounge open to classroom assistants? Is there a work or break room for adult helpers?

Use positive communication and genuine praise.

Be the most positive person you know. Set high expectations for student listening and participation. Use classroom guidelines for answering questions, passing out materials and clean up.

Don't allow put downs or unkind comments. Instead, compliment students on their progress, listening skills, and their respect for others.

Keep your activity moving forward.

Plan ahead. Anticipate student questions and needs so your group will function smoothly.

What you will say to introduce the activity?
How will you keep students engaged in the activity?
How will you handle differences in student work strategies?
How will the activity be concluded?

Carry a pocket activity.

Sometimes a planned activity is completed early or time constraints prevent groups from working on their planned task. Know what to do if this happens.

Do not expect the teacher to provide an activity. Keep a game, book or spare worksheet with your group materials. You may never need it, but you'll be prepared. Use the Hooks to Snag Student Interest page found in the Appendix or on www.PaddyEger. com to jump start your thinking.

Handle transitions.

Problems most often arise when students are in transition to other activities. Some students use the unstructured time to misbehave, push or shove others or otherwise act out.

If you feel you need suggestions for handling such situations, meet with the teacher outside classroom hours. Write down your issues or concerns. Listen and use any suggestions. The teacher is responsible for the classroom and the students. You are there to support both.

Know the policy for leaving students unsupervised.

Safety dictates that students have adult supervision at all times. If you must leave the group, ask another adult to watch over the students until your return.

Practice safe behavior.

- Keep hot drinks out of the classroom.
- Walk, don't run, on the school campus.
- Keep the floor areas uncluttered.
- Move chairs properly, never raised above waist-high.
- Carry scissors properly.
- Open outward-opening doors cautiously.

Treat the teacher's desk as a private space.

Respect the teacher's desk; ask before you handle materials or look for things that may be located there. Personal notes, testing scores, letters from parents or others may be confidential. Ask permission before you begin looking around.

Be positive, helpful, and supportive of the classroom and school.

Every extra adult in a classroom provides much needed hands and minds which translate into extra help for students. Consider these additional ways to provide support:

Volunteer for school-wide activities
Attend programs, concerts, and fundraisers
Support the teacher's goals.
Share special talents, skills, or interests.
Speak to the positive qualities of the school and the teachers.

Put away supplies and materials.

Before leaving an activity, put materials back into their designated place. If you have time, work on small tasks left on the helper desk by the teacher.

Start fresh, each day, with all students.

Move beyond earlier problems and inappropriate student behaviors. Catch students following instructions, behaving appropriately and doing the right thing. Everyone deserves a second, even a third chance.

Maintain confidentiality.

Student performance and behaviors must be kept confidential. Discuss those issues exclusively with the teacher; never with the child, the child's parents or other adults.

If you overhear teacher conversations or see situations where adults are behaving inappropriately towards students, do not repeat what is heard except with the teacher. Such situations need to be handled through proper school channels.

Support teachers by helping with small tasks.

Once teachers become comfortable with their helpers, they discover they can provide additional projects and tasks to the curriculum. Your help frees the teacher to work with one more student, read one more set of papers, or spend extra minutes planning for a new activity.

Leave cell phones and other electronic devices off or on vibrate.

Your attention must stay focused on the students while you are in the classroom. If you are expecting an important call during your work time, arrange for a substitute to cover your classroom duties. Divided focus is unfocused help.

Know you are appreciated by teachers, students and other adults.

Assistants enhanced my classroom in a variety of ways beyond working with small groups. Many helped us develop special activities and projects. To each and every one, thank you.

Examples:

1. We planned a unit on wild animals one year and thought we'd do a program for the fathers. One assistant wrote a song, a poem and a play. Another directed the making of student headbands to be worn while they read their

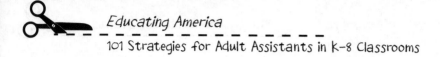

stories aloud. A third created a template for treat bags for the fathers and supervised their construction.

2. The classroom had a series of make-believe stores each spring, creating a chance for students to practice using money. Adult assistants sorted the merchandise, helped students make labels for the various 'shops', assisted students in making change, restocked the shops during the sale hours, as well as helped with set-ups and teardowns. Others made cookies, stuffed beanbags or repotted plants to be sold. Amazing helpers!

3. Most Wednesday afternoons, school handouts arrived from the office and needed to be sent home. By the last recess, assistants collated and sorted them into the student cubbies. We felt a sense of relief and indebtedness to our adult assistants Wednesday after Wednesday after Wednesday.

Mostly for Parents

Parents have special roles when helping in their child's school. In addition to the tips as adult assistants, you, as a parent, have other ways that you can enhance and improve student experiences at school and at home:

Leave your parent hat at the door.
Actively support your child's education.
Establish daily home routines and responsibilities.
Create a 'school place' at home.
Create a homework area.
Establish a homework time for the entire family.
Lead by example.

Leave your parent hat at the door.

Assistants work *for* and *with* all students without ignoring their own children. Talk to your child. Explain the special school job you've taken on, the day and time you'll work at school, and that you're there to help the entire class.

When you arrive at school, be sensitive to your child's needs, but focus on your classroom duties. Speak with individual students beyond your own child. Sit beside your child when it is permitted, but reserve 'cozy sitting' for home.

For young students, your presence may lead to acting-out behavior. If so, you may need to explain your classroom work time goals, rehearse your interactions

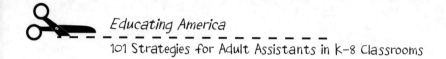

with your child or have the teacher intercede. Students soon learn to appreciate their parent(s) being part of the school day. If issues persist, you may need to strike a deal with your child by setting aside one-on-one time at home that matches your work time at school. That would be a win-win situation.

Leave young siblings with a person away from school unless the teacher gives you permission to bring a sibling along. When you come to work in one child's classroom, a second child may distract you from your task. Babies awaken, preschoolers get restless, sick children fuss and cough. Come alone.

Actively support your child's education.

- Stay informed and involved.
- Participate in school activities, parent groups and workshops.
- Support the teacher's expectations for your child.
- Share your expectations and goals for your child with the teacher during conferences and other appropriate meeting times.
- Share your child's interests, problems and passions, health issues and any changes in home life that might affect school life.
- Read with your child.
- Read school communications, your child's completed work, and homework.
- Post the school calendar along side your child's work.
- Speak to the strengths of the teacher and school.
- Be positive, patient and give praise.

Establish daily home routines and responsibilities.

Start the school day morning with calm activities and a nutritious breakfast. Allow adequate time for your child to wake up, get up, dress, eat and leave for school without rushing around. It's embarrassing and unsettling for kids if they arrive at school with their hair a mess, no lunch, no library book, or no coat.

After school, set aside another calm period. Provide a nutritious snack and allow your child time to read a book or relax before focusing on homework or extracurricular activities.

Start the school morning with calm activities and a nutritious breakfast.

Discuss the day at school. Ask directed questions such as, "What was the best part of math today?" or "What book are you reading at school? Why do you like it?" Actively listen to all answers and ask pertinent, follow-up questions.

Be a positive role model by discouraging conversations that focus on negative activities. If problems arise at school, take your concerns directly to the teacher.

Establish a routine so your child gets enough sleep to ensure a good day tomorrow. Young children need ten hours sleep and middle graders need eight or more hours sleep to be alert and productive the following day.

Think through your child's day. What jobs can your child take on to build confidence and share family responsibilities? Start with:

Feed pets	Empty wastebaskets	Put away clothes
Sweep	Set/Clear the table	Water plants

Each household is different, but every child needs to contribute to their home in preparation for contributing to the classroom and school.

Children need limits. Some decisions like bedtime hour, appropriate meals and TV viewing time belong to parents. But, children can help decide things like what to wear, afternoon snacks and the books to take home from the library.

Student jobs at home builds confidence and share family responsibility.

If your child feels anxious about school, rehearse your morning and after school procedures. Practice getting up on time and getting ready to leave for school. Include having your child pack the school backpack and lunch. After a vacation or long weekend, move your child back to the school schedule as soon as possible.

In the afternoon or evening, homework needs to be completed. Then before bedtime, the backpack is refilled with notes back to the teacher, homework, library books, etc. and placed by the door. The next morning, after your child packs a snack and their lunch, everything is ready. And the best part is that your child handled 'school' with minimal parental guidance.

Starting the school year can be stressful for children. If possible, keep activities to a minimum until the settling-in period is over. Church clubs, youth groups, sports and lessons provide wonderful enriching activities if you also give your child down-time. Everyone of every age needs time to play, read books, relax and use their imaginations in unstructured ways.

Create a 'school place' at home.

Provide a space that is large enough to hold your child's school backpack, school library books, and other school materials. Use a small carpet remnant, a crate, a box or a table by the door. The goal is to encourage your child to take on the responsibility for organizing and transporting homework, library books, notes and such between home and school without parental help.

When your child comes home and puts school things in the 'school place', everything will be easy to locate when it is time to unpack, do homework, etc. After homework is complete, it goes directly into the backpack and is stored in the 'school place', ready for the next day of school.

That next school morning, your child adds the packed lunch, picks up the backpack and other things left at the 'school place' and heads out the door, ready for school. No more calls about forgotten library books and notes; no more "can you bring my picture money?" Responsibility for school is placed squarely on the shoulders of 'the student', not the parent.

Create a "school place" a homework area, and a family homework time

Create a homework area.

Everyone needs a special place for working and doing projects. Your child is no exception. Create a special, quiet, well-lit spot (desk, table, or nook) to store school tools and books. Provide adequate lighting and comfortable seating.

147

For young students it should be quiet but not isolated from the family. When it is time for homework, sit beside your child to get work started. Having a special work area signals your belief that school tasks are important enough to warrant a special place where quality work can be done.

Do the most difficult task first!

Establish a homework time for the entire family.

Everyone needs a time to work on quiet projects at home. This means no TV, distracting music or electronic games. Family homework time is your time to work while your child does school homework. You can pay bills, write letters, sew, read the paper, whatever you need to do for your 'homework.'

During family homework hour, limit phone calls to necessary calls. No exceptions or excuses. When you create a quiet time, you are available to help your child. Good study habits are important skills that families can teach by example.

To start each homework period, discuss the directions. Encourage your child to do the most difficult task first. Check progress every few minutes. Look over the finished work. Help your child decide what revisions would improve the work. If you've made checking work a priority each evening, your child will begin to work more carefully; the need for revisions may reduce after a few weeks.

Don't expect your child to re-do everything on a worksheet completed at school unless the teacher has that expectation. No one enjoys redoing everything every time; that begins to feel like punishment. Instead, select only one or two important items to rework if you believe your child needs reinforcement on a school task.

The most important outcome of daily homework is practicing skills, therefore never do your child's homework. If the tasks are stressing your child, let the teacher know. Adjustments may be possible. Praise each success but remember to tell your child that part of school is learning to see our errors and changing them so we don't make the same mistakes over and over.

Lead by example.

Be an active listener with your child. Use eye contact. Ask higher level thinking questions, such as: "Why did you choose the word 'raced' instead of ran?" "How did you get the answer to this math problem?" "What changes do you think you need to make to improve your answer?"

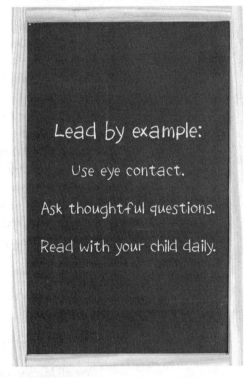

Lead by example:

Use eye contact.

Ask thoughtful questions.

Read with your child daily.

Model a love of learning. Read for information as well as for pleasure. Discuss issues, use resource materials, and talk about what you learn. Read daily to your child and listen to what your child reads to you.

Share your community with your family. Use the neighborhood library, walk through parks, visit museums, attend sporting events, go to art fairs. These activities influence and enrich your family's world.

Limit extra curricular activities for your child during busy times at school. Keep homework time intact and a priority in your family. If you know a large project is due at school, simplify other activities so your child isn't overworked, overtired and too rushed to do a quality thinking on the task.

149

Don't glamorize what you do during the school day. Downplay the activities your child will miss. If you visit "Aunt Mary," your child's favorite relative, expect your child to feel disappointment over not being able to go with you. Don't lie, just explain you had a project to do with Aunt Mary and you spent time working with her. Schedule a fun trip back to visit her outside the school day.

Keep track of your child's progress. Go over all papers brought home. Remember, your child may have spent a long time doing what looks like a simple task. It's your time to actively listen and offer genuine praise as your child shares school. After all, school is your child's work. It's about self-evaluation and small improvements over time and that is important when fostering a love of learning.

Don't accept excuses for work that comes home and reads: "Finish and Return". Look over the task with your child. Help correct errors before sending your child to finish it and return it to school the next school day. Treat each task with respect and give your child time and guidance to finish the work.

Practice patience, praise your child, and share positive comments about school, teachers and classmates. Remember, it's OK:

- To not know all the answers
- To make mistakes
- To try something different
- To ask questions until you understand

We all learn in bits and pieces and over time. Allow your child this same courtesy. Take the time to start age-appropriate routines that will help your child assume responsibility for school.

Appendix

These materials have been designed to improve the way we help students succeed. Although they have been use by numerous adult assistants over the years and proven to be of good value, feel free to adapt them to your specific needs. All of the charts and forms found in this book can be downloaded for FREE from www.PaddyEger.com. Let us know the changes that work when you join in the discussions on the website.

In this Appendix you will find:

Hooks to Snag Student Interest
101+ Jobs Adults Can Do to Assist Teachers
Planning for Adult Assistants
Adult Assistant Inventory
Adult Assistant Task Form (Lesson Plan)
In-Depth Lesson Planning Worksheet
What Can I Do? A guide to Helping in the Classroom
How to Lead a Small Group Activity: Checklist

We wish you the best in all you do as we work together Educating America's children.

HOOKS to Snag Student Interest

Hooks are ways to snag student interest. They are short activities related to the up-coming task. They are intended to grab attention in the first minutes of a small group.

Use a hook to help focus a jittery group or a group that has a difficult time settling in. Use it to build interest in a new activity or to "jazz up" a recurring activity that has become sluggish. The following are a few suggestions to get you started.

General items:
   Theme related games
   Brain Quest style cards
   20 questions game
   Newspaper articles
   Theme books, magazines, poetry, cartoons, puzzles, riddles and jokes
   Artifacts

Language Arts
   Special dictionaries, word books
   Award winning books
   Articles that demonstrate the next topic (verbs, nouns, descriptive words)

Math
   Hands on materials (cubes, tangrams, foam dice, quiet beanbags)
   Card games, flash cards, story problem cards

Social Studies
   Current events
   Maps, globes, atlases

Science
   Touchable objects

Art
   Art prints, artsy note cards, posters, magazines
   Art supplies previously not used

Be ready with the hook when students arrive. Present it with enthusiasm so students will settle down to listen to learn more about it. Hooks are an easy way to re-energize a group or activity.

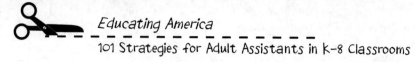

101+ Jobs Adults Can Do
To Assist Teachers

Adults can assist teachers in many ways, from basic chores to leading small groups and designing activities for the classroom. The following suggestions are organized from easiest to those requiring more time, energy and commitment.

Away from School
Cut/assemble projects
Shop for teacher
Create plays, songs, etc.
Edit student writing
Type student writing
Laminate materials

Gather
Materials (shoeboxes, hangers)
Library books
Music, DVD's, art prints
Museum boxes

At School
Sort notes, book orders, mail
Organize picture packets, lunch money
Handle attendance
Hang up/ take down materials
Return borrowed materials
Pass out "go home" materials

Cut out
Bulletin board materials
Project pieces

Walk Students to...
Class
PE/Music/Library
Recess
Assemblies
Cars/Busses
Specialists

Check and Record
Warm up activities
First drafts
Homework
Worksheets
Math problems
Enrichment tasks

Read with Students
One student
Partner readers
Small group
Lunch in the Library

Assist Students
Reading directions
Following directions
Enrichment tasks
Gathering materials
Research materials
Organizing desks
Editing work
Classroom jobs

Clean up
Sharpen pencils
Paints/messy projects
Tables and Bookshelves
Sinks
Science materials
Garbage

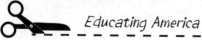
Design and Organize:

Classroom work parties
Rainy day activities
Book Club orders
Field Trip drivers
Field Trip arrangements
Class parties/read-ins
Class picnics/ swim parties
Guest presenters
Mini-course lessons
Newsletters
Bulletin Boards
Class Clubs
    Math
    Literature
    Chess
    News
    Sewing
    Music
    Games
    Recess
Special Projects:
    Themed programs
    Sewing and crafts
    Cooking
    Woodworking
    Read-in
    Art Docent
    Author Study
Fund-raising
Parent Volunteers
Celebrations
Student Store
School Yearbook
Talent/Music Shows

Lead Groups In:

Language Arts
    Dictionary Skills
    Research
    Spelling
    Writer's Workshop
    Literature circles
    Independent Reading
    Editing
Math
    Basic Facts review
    Measurement skills
    Geometry
    Calculator skills
    Story Problems
    Math Games
Science/Health
    Lab Groups
    Projects
    Demonstrations
    Text Discussions
Social Science
    Current Events
    Maps and Globes
    Projects
    Text Discussions
Art/Crafts
    Skill Lessons
    Art Appreciation
    Themed projects
    Gifts
    Sewing
    Cooking
Computer Skills
"Experts"
    Careers
    Gardening
    Artists

Planning for Adult Assistants

Consider the factors below as you include adult assistants in your classroom. Having extra adults working in the classroom is a challenge, but the benefits outweigh the drawbacks. Take your time. Plan out your strategy and enjoy the added support.

Benefits
Improves adult to child ratio
Provides more opportunity to review/reinforce skills
Offers greater chances to enhance learning

Drawbacks
Assistants are not trained educators
Assistant skill levels vary
Assistants may have control problems

Am I Ready to Invite Assistants into my Classroom?

1. Evaluate your style
   What am I willing to allow assistants to handle?
   How much extra planning am I willing to take on?

2. Lay out a plan in detail. Include how to:
   Divide up curriculum lessons for small groups.
   Select tasks organized around basic skills.
   Train assistants for working with students.
   Share the classroom expectations.
   Handle misbehavior.
   Organize and store group materials.
   Track student progress/work, etc.
   Communicate with the assistants during the school day.

   3. Send a letter of invitation and have a meeting.
   Share your educational goals for the class for the year.
   Explain the focus/ tasks for each group.
   Discuss how the small groups will function throughout the day.
   Discuss handling misbehavior and your class rules.
   Share a lesson plan worksheet if assistants will plan for groups.

4. Plan ahead allowing.
   Plan tasks for 3 week periods or longer.
   Create assistant activities requiring minimal supervision.
   Produce notebooks, folders or tubs to organize the tasks.
   Write clear, concise directions.
   Organize group materials, books and supplies.
   Provide a time line for each task.
   Create a feedback plan.

5. Start slowly with 1-2 people a day.
   Prepare all materials and place in an assistant work area.
   Carve out a location where each group will meet.
   Encourage assistants to keep the same jobs for the school year.

6. Shower assistants with sincere praise and thank yous daily.

Educating America Forms © 2011 Paddy Eger www.PaddyEger.com

Adult Assistant Inventory

Name _____ Phone _____

My Background

_____

_____

_____

_____

_____

My interests (circle all that apply)

Reading	Science	Art/Music
Reading Aloud	Experiments	Games
Writing	Math Review	Travel/geography
Language Skills	Math Games	Foreign Language
Publishing	Independent Projects	History
Literature Circles	Careers	News

Other Interests

_____

_____

_____

My strengths

Small groups
Working one on one
Organizational
Other:

_____

_____

Other Comments

_____

_____

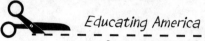

Adult Assistant Task Form
(Lesson Plan)

Group Activity _____ Time: _____

Goals: _____
_____

Supplies needed: _____
_____
_____

Directions:
1. _____
_____
2. _____
_____
3. _____
_____
4. _____
_____
5. _____
_____
6. _____
_____

Remember...Check off each part of the task:
- Give clear, concise directions
- After 5 minutes, remind the students of the task objectives
- Observe student work during the time period and help where needed
- Give a 5-minute warning before ending student work time
- Allow time for cleanup by the students
- End with a brief review of today's task
- Dismiss the students with control

Concerns:
_____
_____
_____

Adult Helper Name _____ Date _____

In Depth Lesson Planning Worksheet

Content area _____ Dates _____

Task: _____

Level of Understanding:
___exposure/new concept ___review ___practice ____enrichment ___assessment

Specific Objective: _____

    Materials: _____

Time Allotment: 3-5 minute intro + _____minute lesson + 3-6 minute cleanup/ closure

Introduction (related to task objective)
    ___ media (picture book, poem, photo, short text, drawing, TV, map, book)

    ___ "hook" (puzzle, riddle, question, observation, relevant object)

    ___ review (question, brief activity, game, true-false, discussion)

    ___ activity (worksheet, puzzle, research, drawing, "word of the day")

    ___ resume previously started activity

Brief explanation of task for students:

_____

_____

Work Strategy
    ___ work alone ___ work with partner ___ group task ___share answers

Quality Level:
    ___ practice ___ working paper ___ final copy ___ rubric scoring ___ assessment

Date Due:
    ___ today ___ next meeting time ___as able to complete ___ specific date:_____

Check Understanding
    — 5 minutes into task ___ group reminder each session ___ individual assistance

Closure:
    ___ share work ___ discussion ___ plan the next step ___ other: _____

Clean-up:
    ___ assign student jobs ___ all help ___ special: _____

Evaluation:
__ self correct __ send home __ adult correct __ teacher correct __ assessment

Extensions/Enrichments:
_____
_____

Suggestions/Comments/Questions
_____
_____

Reminders:
__clean up __ pocket activity __ note to teacher __ work copies needed?

What Can I Do?
A Guide to Helping in the Classroom

When you have a free moment before activities or explanations begin OR after you complete your activity....
<u>Remember, your assigned task comes first.</u>

WITH STUDENTS during opening, seat work or work time
> Assist students with directions
> Listen to children (talking about a task, dictation, sharing ideas).
> Read TO or WITH students
> Supervise students working at centers, tables, etc.

Clean the sink
> Wash out brushes, containers and vases; put away.
> Wash cups, dishes and water bottles; put away

Look at the floor
> Pick up papers, books, etc.
> Check for tripping items; make areas safer

Check out centers
> Straighten books in library
> Straighten materials after reading the directions
> Reattach bulletin board items, directions
> Put away "stray items" that belong elsewhere
> Replenish center and shared supplies

Check student tables
> Sponge off glue, paste, paint and markers(leave the table dry and usable)
> Reattach names and other tags on tables

Check student shelves
> Pick up student backpacks, clothing, etc. that has fallen off the hooks
> Put student mail, papers in appropriate place

Check adult desk or work area
> Sort and hand out student work, newsletters, etc
> Take collected items (Campbell labels, labels for education) to drop site
> Sort out items for office, etc. and deliver if there is time
> Cut, collate, staple, band, correct, etc. as indicated by the teacher's notes
> File materials

IF STUDENTS ARE OUT OF THE ROOM:
> Vacuum floor (corners and behind centers)
> Wipe down chairs and tables
> Clean white board (If using chemical spray be sure students are out 30 minutes;
> Air out the room. ASK teacher what to leave on the board
> Hang art on hooks over student areas
> Sort out blocks, etc
> Remove sticky tape from windows doors and walls. Clean off residue

How to Lead a Small Group Activity: Checklist

1. Come to the classroom prepared.
- Understand the specific task to be done.
- Arrive on time.
- Collect and organize needed materials.
- Know where to meet and work with the students.
- Bring energy and a calm demeanor to leading the group

2. Seat yourself strategically within the group
- Sit in the best position for control and positive interaction.
- Avoid sitting at the "head" of the table.

3. Establish yourself as leader of the group
- Model and share your expectations.
- Explain your signals for student participation.
- Give students clear directions.
- Use "wait time" and open ended questions.

4. Keep students focused during activities.
- Confirm student understanding of the task after 5 minutes.
- Check student progress throughout the work period.
- Modify work to match student abilities.
- Keep track of students leaving your group (rest room, etc.).
- Praise quality work; encourage personal best.
- Plan a movement or refocusing activity if the group is restless.

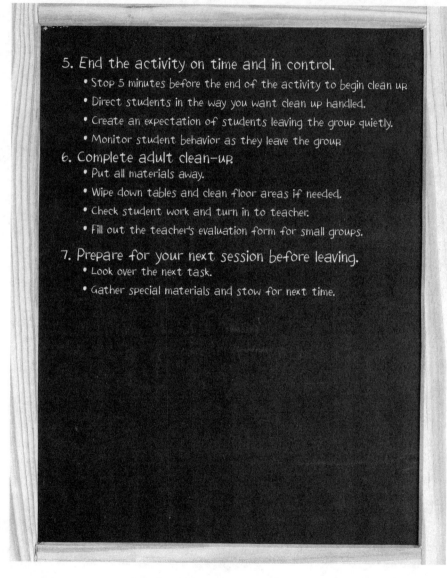

5. End the activity on time and in control.
   • Stop 5 minutes before the end of the activity to begin clean up.
   • Direct students in the way you want clean up handled.
   • Create an expectation of students leaving the group quietly.
   • Monitor student behavior as they leave the group.

6. Complete adult clean-up.
   • Put all materials away.
   • Wipe down tables and clean floor areas if needed.
   • Check student work and turn in to teacher.
   • Fill out the teacher's evaluation form for small groups.

7. Prepare for your next session before leaving.
   • Look over the next task.
   • Gather special materials and stow for next time.

How to Lead a Small Group Activity: Checklist con't.

Glossary

Closure: to sum up a task before moving on to another: "What did you learn?" "Tell us one thing you remember about..."

Confidentiality: keeping important information about students private

Expectations: the criteria students are taught to follow

Focusing questions: guidelines to help students organize to do their best work

Hook: brief, high interest activity that captures student attention

Manipulatives: hands on objects like blocks, cubes, globes and maps, etc.

Misbehavior: actions that disrupt and distract students from their work

Personal best: the best quality of work a person can do at the present time

Pocket activity: a simple game, book, idea used to fill in free work time

Prior knowledge: background information and ideas students bring to current experiences

Quality of printing/writing: the current level or stage of personal writing skills

Quality of thought: the current level or stage of personal thinking skills

Rubric: detailed information about the expectations of the work to be done on a task.

Signals: ways to let students know your expectations and procedures

Wait time: the delay between asking questions and accepting answers that allows students time to think and evaluate their answers

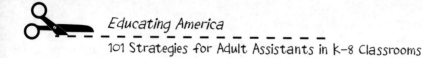

Index

M

misbehavior four-step plan 63-67, 71

monitor (students and work) 24, 70-73, 89-103, 112, 125-126

O

offices 15, 18

off-task behavior 25, 61, 63, 66, 70, 72, 89, 99-100, 129

open-ended questions 41, 110-111

P

partner work 9, 22, 82, 130, 135-136

personal best 31, 93, 98, 113, 116-117

planning 36, 119, 124, 125-127, 131, 133, 136-137, 141, 157, 163

pocket activity 8, 9, 100, 136, 138

practice skills 9, 34, 44, 48, 62, 75, 81, 94-95, 107, 114-115, 123, 142

Q

quality of thought 105, 113-115

questioning strategies 47-59, 134

R

respect 4, 15, 21-22, 28, 74, 88, 112, 137-138, 150

responsibility 7-8, 11, 28-29, 66, 74-75, 91, 119, 121, 146-147, 149-150

rubrics 90-92, 107

S

school place 143, 147

seating 14, 19, 27-28, 65

signals 33, 37-41, 66-68

strategies 47-59, 134, 138

T

thinking skills 9, 34, 37-38, 41, 47, 49-52, 54, 73, 81-88, 98-100, 110-111, 113-114, 122, 131, 134, 149

think-pair-share 47, 49

thumb up 39, 52, 57, 68, 110, 122

V

voice level 15, 17, 22, 24-25, 34, 36, 65, 72, 106, 112, 128

wait time 38-39, 47, 50, 52, 58, 69, 88, 109-110

About the Author

Paddy Eger is a veteran teacher from the Edmonds School District 15 in Washington state. She's participated in classrooms as a community volunteer, a parent volunteer, a parent trainer as well as a teacher in primary and intermediate grades.

Her years in the PCEP, the Parent Cooperative Education Program, as teacher and trainer created the basis for the book, *Educating America: 101 Strategies for Adult Assistants in K-8 Classrooms*. All the practices, suggestions and examples grew out of actual use by Paddy, other teachers, parent helpers and other adult assistants.

Paddy graduated from the University of Washington with a degree in elementary education. An interest in teaching began in sixth grade when she 'taught' spelling to her classmates. Her dedication to children and her profession has resulted in her receiving two awards: a *PTA Golden Acorn* and *Teacher of the Month* from her local educational association.

Paddy is a Washington native. She and her husband have two adult children. They divide their time between Edmonds and Hood Canal and enjoy international travel as well.

In her free time, Paddy enjoys writing children's books, reading, editing others writing and creating fiber art pieces. She is walking an imaginary perimeter of the USA; thinking about our vast country helps when it's a wet western Washington day.

For information on training workshops and speaker presentations contact the author at her website: www.PaddyEger.com.

"With a little training and a handful of strategies, most adults can successfully assist teachers in guiding students along their educational paths."

—P.Eger

Order More Today!

Online orders: www.TendrilPress.com

Mail Postal Orders to:

Tendril Press, LLC PO Box 441110 Aurora, CO 80044

Quantity orders discounts please call: 303.696.9227

The price of each book is $14.95 plus applicable taxes.

Discounts available for quantity orders

USA shipping —$4.75 for the first book,
+ $1.50 for each additional book.

International shipping is $10.00 for the first book,
$5.00 for each additional book,

US Check or Major Credit Cards accepted.

Card number: _____

Name on card: _____

Exp. Date: _____ CVC2 Code: _____

Signature: _____

Telephone: _____

Ship to:

Name: _____

Address: _____

City: _____ State: _____ Zip: _____

Email Address: _____

Telephone: _____

New Releases and Top Sellers
from Tendril Press

   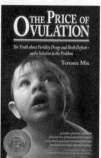

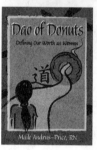  

Tendril Press, LLC, is an Independent Press,
publishing thought provoking, educational, inspirational and
humanitarian books for adults and children.
Our highly-selective process is paying off, as we have multiple
award-winning books and an accepted entry for the Pulitzer Prize
We are changing lives worldwide, one book at a time.
Visit us often at *www.TendrilPress.com*
For Quantity order of any title please call
303.696.9227